THE HAMPTON PRESS COMMUNICATION SERIES

Interpersonal Communication

Don Cegala, Editor

The Biology of Communication: A Communibiological Perspective
Michael J. Beatty and James C. McCroskey

Avoiding Communication (Second Edition)
John A. Daly, James C. McCroskey, Joe Ayres, Tim Hopf, and Debbie M. Ayres (eds.)

Imagined Interactions: Daydreaming About Communication
James M. Honeycutt

Communication and Personality: Trait Perspectives
James C. McCroskey, John A. Daly, Matthew M. Martin, and Michael J. Beatty

Identity Matters: Communication-Based Explorations and Explanations
Hartmut B. Mokros (ed.)

Conflict and Gender
Anita Taylor and Judi Beinstein Miller (eds.)

IMAGINED INTERACTIONS

DAYDREAMING ABOUT COMMUNICATION

JAMES M. HONEYCUTT
LOUISIANA STATE UNIVERSITY

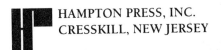

HAMPTON PRESS, INC.
CRESSKILL, NEW JERSEY

Printed in the United States of America

Library of Congress Cataloging-in-Publication Data

Honeycutt, James M..
    Imagined interactions : daydreaming about communication / James M. Honeycutt.
      p. cm. -- (Interpersonal communication)
    Includes bibliographical references and indexes.
    ISBN 1-57273-413-2 (c) -- ISBN 1-57273-414-0 (p)
     1. Social interaction. 2. Imagination. 3. Fantasy. I. Title. II. Series.

HM1111 .H66 2002
302--dc21   2002068924

Hampton Press, Inc.
23 Broadway
Cresskill, NJ 07626

This book is dedicated to my family,
Frank and Arletha Honeycutt, my parents,
and my brother, Frank III, and Susan.
They were there.

CONTENTS

PREFACE

While going to work and waiting in traffic, individuals may recall conversations they had with friends while anticipating what they will say for future encounters. Before a job interview, the interviewee may rehearse in his or her mind what the interviewer may ask and how to respond. After an argument with a romantic partner, people may replay the conversation and feel despair at not having said various things that are currently in their mind. In the first scenario, a proactive imagined interaction has occurred, whereas in the second a retroactive imagined interaction has occurred. It is also possible that the retroactive encounter in the second scenario acts as preinteraction stimulus for the next encounter with the romantic partner.

Imagined interactions (IIs) are a type of daydreaming in which individuals think about conversations in their minds. IIs are attempts to simulate real-life conversations with others (Honeycutt, 1991; Honeycutt, Edwards, & Zagacki, 1989-1990; Honeycutt, Zagacki, & Edwards, 1989). Mead (1934) described internal conversations in terms of self-concept development in which individuals assume the perspective of others to understand the self. We respond to ourselves by taking the role of others, imagining how they might respond to one's messages within particular situations, and thus test and imagine the consequences of alternative messages prior to communication (Edwards, Honeycutt, & Zagacki, 1988; Honeycutt, 1991; Zagacki, Edwards, & Honeycutt, 1992).

This book is about the characteristics and functions of IIs. Like real conversations, IIs may be fragmentary, extended, rambling, repetitive, or coherent. They may occur during the course of a day or while waiting to fall asleep.

A variety of functions in everyday life are served by imagined interactions. Functions include rehearsing for important conversations (e.g., job interview), analyzing and understanding one's position on a variety of issues, maintaining relationships by thinking about someone who is important in our lives while out of his or her physical presence, managing conflict by reliving old arguments, compensating for the lack of real interaction with someone by thinking about the person, and catharsis in which emotions are expressed, including repressed anger as well as feelings of joy and happiness.

From a theoretical viewpoint, IIs provide a mechanism to operationalize the study of intrapersonal communication—the study of internal communication as it affects communication in interpersonal relationships. From a practical viewpoint, I believe that studying and understanding IIs can help people prepare for actual conversational encounters and provide insight into problems affecting individuals with interpersonal relationships.

ORGANIZATION OF THE BOOK

Chapter 1 reviews some of the research on components of daydreaming. The theoretical foundation of IIs in terms of symbolic interactionism and cognitive scripts is discussed. Different modes of imagery are used including visual and verbal imagery while imagining conversation. The timing of IIs in relation to actual conversations is discussed as well as differences between IIs and fantasy.

Chapter 2 describes eight characteristics of IIs. There are individual differences in how much each characteristic reflects IIs. For example, women report having more IIs than men, and people high in loneliness tend to report having fewer IIs. However, when lonely people imagine conversations, they tend to be discrepant from what actually occurs during real conversations.

Chapter 3 discusses functions of IIs. The functions may occur in combination as well as independently. The functions are relationship maintenance, managing conflict, rehearsing messages for anticipated encounters, self-understanding, catharsis or emotional release, and compensating for the lack of real interaction.

Chapters 4 and 5 elaborate on two of these functions in more detail due to their importance and the prevalence of research in these functions. Chapter 4 discusses how IIs maintain relationships. For example, in long-distance romantic relationships, individuals often imagine talking with their relational partner.

Chapter 5 discusses how conflict is managed in terms of dwelling on arguments as well as being resolved through recall of prior arguments while anticipating future encounters. Sometimes people rehearse what they might say in their minds while preparing for an anticipated argument. People also replay what was said and link a series of conversations together such that themes of conflict are discovered. For example, someone who describes their relationship as *stormy* may recall heated episodes of arguing.

Chapter 6 discusses cross-cultural characteristics and functions of IIs in Japan and Thailand compared with the United States. The relationship between II characteristics and cultural patterns of horizontal versus vertical individualism and collectivism are discussed. IIs among foreign students who are temporarily residing in the United States for higher education are discussed. The IIs of Chinese students following the Tian-an-men Square demonstration are discussed.

Chapter 7 consists of studies of imagined interactions in a variety of contexts. Studies of IIs during forensic competition and debates are reviewed as well as IIs in managing cancer. IIs among homeless women are investigated. Research examining IIs among banking executives is reviewed, as well as similarities and differences between IIs and prayer and the use of IIs in detecting deception. Speculations for future inquiries into the importance of imagined interactions in various contexts are also presented.

The final chapter provides a practical guide to enhancing communication effectiveness and self-confidence through IIs. The therapeutic benefits of daydreaming and IIs are discussed. Tips for having better IIs are presented as well as a list of things to avoid in constructing more productive messages. Each of the characteristics of IIs is discussed in relation to producing more effective messages.

—James M. Honeycutt

ACKNOWLEDGMENTS

This book would not be possible without the inspiration and assistance of a number of people. I thank Professor Don Cegala, also a fellow drummer of the Ohio State University. His comments on earlier drafts were very helpful and insightful.

I thank my research assistants, Amy Maddox and Jill McLaurin, for helping with various imagined interaction (II) projects. I thank Bob McCann for our intense discussions on daydreaming and IIs when we were together in California and Thailand. He inspired me in the cross-country analyses. I thank Dr. Michael Eidenmuller for his interest in music therapy and imagined interactions. He and I also played the keyboards and drums, respectively in recording sessions. We had many discussions about the therapeutic uses of IIs and their role in enhancing communication competence.

I thank Heather Dufau, a research assistant from Santa Cruz, who helped code data on IIs and daydreaming while I was a visiting professor at the University of California at Santa Barbara. I acknowledge the following graduate students: Jing Liu, Tiwa Saechou, Charles Choi, Jow Mitchell, and Jon Croghan for their interest in the cross-cultural extension of IIs. Special thanks go to Sherry Ford for assisting with the literature review on the functions of IIs. Finally, I am thrilled with the continuing research of Professor Dominique Gendrin of Xavier University in New Orleans. She has studied IIs among homeless women, different types of marriages, and among immigrants in the United States using IIs to assist in learning English as a second language.

I acknowledge the inspiration of my former band members, Dr. Fernando Figueroa and Thomas Couvillon. We had philosophical discussions about imagination, values, and temperament. They provided catharsis and promoted the self-understanding function of IIs in me. The discussions were as stimulating as the music.

I also thank the numerous students I have had who have discussed their IIs and daydreams in journal reports and during class. They have always been fascinated with imagined interactions. Finally, I appreciate the support and encouragement of Elizabeth and two of my colleagues at LSU, Dr. Andrew King and Dr. Hugh Buckingham.

Chapter 1

DAYDREAMING ABOUT COMMUNICATION
THROUGH IMAGINED INTERACTIONS

Every day we imagine conversations with friends, business associates, and even people we despise in which prior conversations are replayed in our minds. We have imagined interactions (IIs) anticipating encounters in which we rehearse what we will say. Imagining conversations is a type of daydreaming. IIs serve a number of functions including rehearsing conversations, making sense of what has already occurred, engaging in fantasies, and stimulating us for repetitive actions.

This book is about our inner world of communication and how we often imagine talking with others who are important in our lives. We can recall instances in which we imagined saying something to others while never saying the imagined statements, as well as instances in which we said what we rehearsed. Often we replay conversations after they occurred and imagine various outcomes if we had said something other than what was actually stated.

DEFINITION OF IMAGINED INTERACTIONS

IIs are pervasive in everyday life. For example, while driving to work, you could imagine conversations you will be having later in the day at work. Hardly a day passes without some type of daydreaming about communication. The

1

notion of IIs is derived from work in intrapersonal communication and symbolic interaction. *Imagined interaction* refers to a process of social cognition whereby actors imagine and therefore indirectly experience themselves in anticipated and/or past communicative encounters with others (Honeycutt et al., 1989, 1989-1990). Imagined interactions are a type of social cognition in which communicators experience cognitive representations of conversation with accompanying verbal and nonverbal features. Imagined interactions focus and organize individuals' thoughts on communication—on the actors involved in specific acts of communication and on the communicative context.

Imagined interactions occur when we think about talking with someone we know or expect to encounter. For example, you may imagine what to tell a traffic cop after being pulled over for speeding as she approaches your car. You may also have been thinking about a prior conversation with someone while speeding and became engrossed in the imaging process. Imagined interactions recognize that there are other persons in the interaction setting such that some degree of projection as well as thinking about the perspective of others exists. Imagined interactions are not simply instances of self-talk such as rehearsing a speech or talk, which is a monologue as opposed to dialogue.

Figure 1.1 reveals the symbolic location of imagined interactions within the human mind. We imagine what another communicator may say or replay what he or she said. Imagined interactions are attempts to simulate real-life

---

FIG. 1.1. Symbolic location of IIs within the human mind.

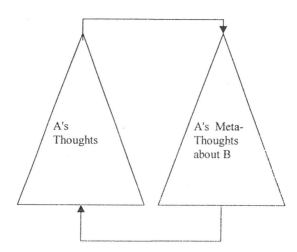

"A's" IIs occur within his or her mind as signified by the box. A's thoughts reflect what he or she may say to "B." "A's" meta-thoughts about B reflect what "A" imagines that "B" says to "A." The arrows represent the exchanged messages that are imagined.

conversations with significant others. One can actually envision participation in discourse with others, anticipate their response, and even assume their roles. Although imagined interactions may not fully picture the context of actual (or recalled) conversation, we believe individuals can accurately represent many of the physical and socioemotional elements that are part of a real interaction. However, there are instances where real encounters radically depart from their imagined predecessors. Thus, imagined interactions should be conceived as an extension of intrapersonal communication and as a specific type of social cognition in which communicators experience cognitive representations of conversation with its accompanying verbal and nonverbal features. In the parlance of cognitive theorists, imagined interactions are perhaps best related to what Greene (1984) called *procedural records*—cognitive structures that provide cues for rehearsing and/or reviewing interaction. Procedural records specify various communicative actions that are associated with accomplishing goals.

IIs are a mindful as opposed to a mindless activity (Honeycutt, 1991). Langer, Blank, and Chanowitz (1978) demonstrated how individuals process information mindlessly in which they do not carefully attend to information in their immediate environment. There is an absence of flexible cognitive processing. Mindlessness occurs when the individual relies on old, established ways of thinking. Mindlessness is a type of perception that is rigid to the extent that individuals rely on previous distinctions (Langer, Chanowitz, & Blank, 1985). In contrast, mindfulness implies creative thought and attention to information. Mindfulness enables one to make distinctions and create categories. Individuals are likely to be mindful or engaging in thought when encountering novel situations for which no script can be utilized (Langer, 1989). IIs play a role here by envisioning contingency plans for actions in which the confidence that a given plan is initiated is low.

THEORETICAL FOUNDATION OF IIS

Imagined interactions have their theoretical foundation in the work of symbolic interactionists and phenemonologists, especially Mead (1934), Dewey (1922), and Schutz (1962). Mead discussed the "internalized conversation of gestures." Here actors are consciously able to monitor social action by reviewing alternative endings of any given act in which they are involved. Actors use internal dialogues to "test out implicitly the various possible completions of an already initiated act in advance of actual completion of the act," and thus to choose "the one which it is most desirable to perform explicitly or carry into overt effect" (p. 177). Communication scholars have described intrapersonal communication as what Mead (1934) called the "internalized conversation of gestures" (p. 173).

Mead cited an individual's ability to monitor social action as a distinguishing mark of human intelligence. He showed that individuals can have present, "in terms of attitudes or implicit responses, the alternative possible overt completions of any given act in which we are involved" (p. 117). The individual can "test out implicitly the various possible completions of an already initiated act in advance of actual completion of the act," and thus choose "the one which it is most desirable to perform explicitly or carry into overt effect" (p. 117). This process pertains, in part, to what Mead called the individual's *internal conversation* with him or herself. These internal dialogues could involve taking the role of others to see ourselves as others see us. As Mead (1934) illustrated, "One separates the significance of what he is saying to other from the actual speech and gets it ready before saying it. He thinks it out, and perhaps writes it in the form of a book" (p. 118). This sort of precommunicative mental activity, explained Manis and Meltzer (1978), "is a peculiar type of activity that goes on in the experience of the person. The activity is that of the person responding to himself, of indicating things to himself" (p. 21). Mead noted that such activity is essential to the constitution of the self: "That the person should be responding to himself is necessary to the self, and it is this sort of social conduct which provides behavior within which that self appears" (p. 118). What is important about this type of mental activity is that (a) one may consciously take the role of others, imagining how they might respond to one's messages within particular situations; and thus (b) one can test and imagine the consequences of alternative messages prior to communication.

When we communicate with others, we have an understanding of what is being said by the symbols created over time. When having imagined interactions, we use the same symbols that are used in social communication, which makes it possible for us to express our ideas outward in a meaningful way. Thus, our minds are an internalized form of symbolic interaction. Our access of symbols also allows us to plan and imagine future events because the symbols remain constant.

Schutz (1962) described Dewey's notion of deliberation as a planning activity that precedes action; actors plan by imagining a future instance where an action will have already been accomplished "and reconstruct[ing] the future steps which will have brought forth this future act" (p. 69). For Schutz (1962), deliberation is "a dramatic rehearsal in imagination of various competing possible lines of action" (p. 69). Hence, in their intrapersonal experience, individuals imagine desirable and undesirable future states of events and imagine ways to obtain or avoid these states (Honeycutt & Ford, 2001). IIs provide a means by which to plan conversations using visual and verbal imagery.

In discussing cognitive editing, Meyer (1997) described the process of message formulation, which occurs as an individual activates a message goal—such as asking for a favor—and recalls appropriate situational schema. The individual may find it necessary to mentally rehearse a message to assess its potential impact on relational outcomes prior to actually transmitting the message. This mental rehearsal enables one to detect potential problems prior to message production—an important tool for competent communicators and key to the functioning of imagined interactions. Hence, in their subjective experience, actors envision desirable and undesirable future states of affairs and imagine ways to obtain or avoid these states.

In addition to their planning capacity, we can speculate that IIs are related to cognitive structures similar to interaction schema and procedural records (Edwards et al., 1988; Honeycutt et al., 1989; Zagacki et al., 1992). Cognitive theorists have posited that procedural knowledge for real-world events and actions is inscribed into cognitive structures (Berger, 1988; Greene, 1984; Schank, 1982) yet they have spent little time speculating about how this knowledge is accessed and consequently experienced within phenomenal awareness or direct consciousness.

Wenberg and Wilmot (1973) claimed that "Ultimately, all communication responses take place within persons as we react to various communication cues . . . intrapersonal communication provides the basis for all other communication arenas" (p. 21). They suggested that "intrapersonal communication is the communication with oneself. Within this arena, one receives signals that characterize one's own feelings or sensations" (p. 20). Likewise, Roloff and Berger (1982) discussed how that intrapersonal communication and social cognition involves the use of representational systems, focuses on certain aspects of interaction (e.g., self, others, or behaviors), and has some impact on behavior.

Rosenblatt and Meyer (1986) applied Mead's notion to counseling situations. They posited the existence of imagined interactions, suggesting that they "may occur in self-controlled daydreams, or they may occur as the mind wanders" (p. 319). Imagined interactions may possess many of the traits of real conversations: They may be fragmentary, extended, rambling, repetitive, or coherent. Actors within IIs might control conversations or relinquish control to the imagined others. IIs frequently occur during the course of an actor's day. Most involve actors in conversations with significant others, such as family members, close friends, intimates, or work partners.

In terms of everyday living, IIs refer to a process of social cognition whereby actors imagine themselves in interaction with others. IIs may precede, follow, or even help constitute the decision-making process. Brook's notion that intrapersonal communication involves talking to ourselves is important because not only do individuals talk to themselves, but during IIs they talk to others as well. Thus, IIs are an extended form of intrapersonal communication.

DIFFERENCES BETWEEN IIS AND SELF-TALK

IIs should not be confused with self-talk as monologue. Klinger (1990) reported that the single most common feature of daydreams is self-talk. He provided an example of hearing sounds and saying, "What the heck is that?" (p. 68). Klinger reported on beeper studies in which individual carried electronic beepers that beeped at various times of the day. The individuals spoke into a microcassette recorder about what they were thinking. He found that when the research participants were beeped, inner voices in the form of self-talk were completely quiet in only 25% of their thoughts.

IIs involve dialogue with another interaction partner. Self-talk is speaking only to ourselves. Roloff and Ifert (1998) discussed private speech. Private speech occurs when individuals talk aloud to themselves, and this may occur in isolation or in the presence of others. When it occurs in the presence of others, there is the absence of nonverbal or linguistic cues indicating to others that the speech is not directed to them. Vygotsky (1986) believes that private speech helps individuals self-regulate themselves as they talk through a task or problem with themselves and guides individuals in their current and future behavior. Over time, private speech moves from being vocalized to a silent, internal monologue that individuals carry on with themselves.

Most IIs occur outside of the imagined party's physical presence. Sometimes IIs occur during a live conversation when we anticipate what another might say next. This is referred to as *online IIs*. This is discussed further in chapter 5 when discussing arguments and conflict management. We tend to listen or decode messages faster than we speak, so sometimes we go back and replay prior comments made by the interaction partner as well as possibly anticipating ensuing messages. Box 1.1 contains a sample report from a former student who reported offline and online IIs with a dean about the problems faced by minority students in one of the colleges because of lack of minority professors and staff. The meeting occurred with the dean and local representatives of the NAACP.

BOX 1.1

Sample II Reflecting Online and Offline Imaging

Topic: Lack of minority faculty and staff in a college

At a recent meeting with the dean of the school of mass communication, I experienced many online and offline IIs. The meeting was important because it was the first time the dean sat down and listened to our concerns. Before the meeting, I had IIs because I wanted to ensure that the most important issues were addressed at the meeting. I was thinking about the dean's response. I wanted to make sure that I knew what I wanted to say and to sound intelligent.

The usual excuse to our argument was that there was a small pool of minorities to choose from and the school could not afford to hire them. This excuse infuriates me because this is the media's excuse as a whole. In my mind, I had IIs about what I would say if this were his answer to my question about minority faculty and staff. I imagined him telling me this excuse and replying that the school uses lots of money recruiting international students but it will not use this extra money to keep the students it already has.

I also imagined asking him why the school did not offer any minority guest speakers. I imagined his response would be that there is a small pool of minority professionals. I imagined myself responding with the fact that there are many minorities that hold prominent positions in mass communications in Baton Rouge. I imagined that the dean would patronize the group with "what do you want me to do about it" answers to our heart-felt concerns.

When I arrived at the actual meeting, I found out that the meeting would accomplish little. I asked the first question: Everyone acts as if there are only 10 good minority journalists in the entire nation and this is why you don't have minorities on the staff. I find this hard to believe, so what are you are going to do about the lack of minorities in the school? After asking the question, I immediately had an online II anticipating that he was going to feed me a bunch of garbage. The next few sentences out of his mouth proved me right. He affirmed this myth. I sat there thinking, "I can't believe he is really going to sit here and tell us this is the reason why there is no minority faculty and staff besides the janitor."

The next imagined lines of dialogue I experienced were not pleasant. I imagined telling him that what he was saying was *bull*, I would not give the school one red cent after I graduate, and that the school did not think enough of me as a student to address some important concerns to myself and other minorities. Of course, I imagined him getting defensive and leaving the meeting, so I kept my composure and started thinking about my next question.

While others asked different question, I thought of the possible answers that the dean could give to my next question: Why doesn't the school ever invite minority speaker's to come and speak at the school? His answer was a little surprising. He said that he understood that concern and he would try and improve that in the future.

I had both online and offline IIs concerning this meeting. This experience gave me self-understanding. After the meeting, I understood that change takes time, I just do not understand why change is still taking so much time. Although change may be slow, there are individuals who have to take the initiative and speed up the change process. After the meeting, I felt I had expressed my concerns intelligently and in a nonoffensive manner. I feel that although this meeting might not bring a lot of change, at least we took the first step. This was just the beginning of a series of several steps that lead to a change in the school.

Most IIs occur outside of the physical presence of the other interactants. As Allen and Honeycutt (1997) noted, "Off-line, individuals may imagine what they believe is reasonable in light of past experiences and what they believe is most likely to occur" (p. 68). Yet online planning does occur although it is cognitively debilitating because an ongoing conversation is happening as well as attempting to process what may have already been said or anticipating what is to come. Allen and Honeycutt discussed how contingency planning (online) is cognitively inefficient. Furthermore, Bratman (1987) discussed how people have limited resources for attending to problems, deliberating about options, determining possible consequences, and performing contingencies. Offline IIs provide an opportunity for problem solving prior to devising an actual plan for action because individuals can use IIs to test contingencies (Allen & Honeycutt, 1997).

DAYDREAMING AND IMAGINED INTERACTIONS

An II is a type of daydream that is prevalent in everyday life. Giambra (1980) studied more than 1,300 people and found that 94% of college students reported daydreaming at least once a day, most of them many times a day. Moreover, the characteristics of daydreams are similar to actual sensation.

Imagining conversations use brain neurotransmitters similar to those used when we observe something or engage in a behavior. Klinger (1990) noted that (a) we can be fooled into confusing mental images with external ones; (b) imagining something makes it harder to see something real, unless it happens to be the same stimulus you are imagining; (c) brain areas active in seeing are also active in visualizing; and (d) injury to the brain knocks out the ability to see certain things and eliminates the ability to imagine the objects.

Many of our daydreams focus on what is currently happening. For example, Mariah is listening to a lecture on self-talk and wishes the lecturer would finish so she could go study for a few extra minutes for a test she has the next period. Yet as shown in Fig. 1.2, 24% of our IIs are concerned with past conversations (retroactive IIs) or anticipated interactions (proactive IIs). Insofar as the timing of daydreams are concerned in relation to the here and now, almost 30% of the time we pay attention to what we are doing or what is happening around us (Klinger, 1990). These do not necessarily involve IIs. An additional third of the time, our daydreams are concerned with surrounding contextual elements in terms of the things going on around us in our setting. Finally, 14% of our daydreams have no time element relative to the past, current, or future. These daydreams also include recurring conversations or general subjects that transcend time although imagined interactions may or may not be experienced here.

Despite common beliefs about daydreams and sexual fantasies, less than 1% but no more than 5% of the daydreams are concerned with sex. Klinger (1990) reported that among our daydreams, we tend to be thinking about other people and relationships. Most of our daydreams are concerned with issues and problems in our lives, people we know, and reflections about their states. Indeed, as noted in more detail in the next chapter, many of the topics of imagined interactions deal with these issues.

FIG. 1.2. Timing of daydreams and IIs.

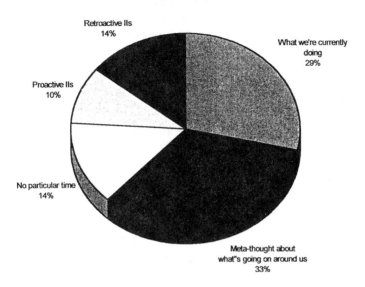

Klinger (1990) had students carry beepers; when the students were beeped, they reported what they were thinking about by filling out a diary or speaking into a minicassette recorder. More than 25% of the students' thoughts involved IIs in which they speculated on an interaction partner's mood or how the partner might feel about some issues.

Klinger (1990) reported that only 3% of daydreams are concerned with stress or anxiety-provoking thoughts. Imagining conversations about anxiety reflect failure in some area, such as being rejected by a lover or imagining events that take some kind of undesirable turn. We imagine discussing fears and vulnerabilities. Klinger provided the following example in which a man links the past and future by recalling a brief affair he had had with his manager's wife. The man imagines that the women spites him by telling her husband. The man imagines a number of scenarios about the boss' angry reactions. These scenes terrify him as he imagines losing his job. Although daydreaming may be associated with anxiety, numerous benefits of imagining encounters exist and are discussed in chapter 8.

IIS AS OPERANT THOUGHT

IIs may be viewed as a type of operant thought process. Klinger (1981) discussed operant thought as a problem–solution analysis in which one analyzes issues confronting the self. IIs used for message planning reflect this process. Klinger

(1978, 1981) also discussed respondent thought. This type of thought involves all other types of cognition and IIs not used for message planning. Most of what we consider daydreams, dreams, and fantasies are respondent thought.

Operant thought is concerned with problem solution, analysis of an issue confronting one, and is active rather than passive. It is volitional as it is checked against new information concerning its effectiveness in moving toward a resolution. Operant thought involves a higher level of mental activity.

IIs may be experienced in the form of what Abelson (1976) originally referred to as *vignettes*. These are representations of short-duration events that are similar to a panel in a cartoon strip where a visual image is accompanied by a verbal caption. Honeycutt (1991) indicated that the metaphor of a cartoon reader is important in revealing the rehearsal function of IIs because an individual having an II "is afforded the luxury of moving back and forth over the panel, even "rewriting" the strip if appropriate" (p. 127). Just as cartoons contain visual and verbal information, IIs may use both types of imagery. Furthermore, interactors may possess, like cartoon characters, power over the imagined conversation (e.g., topic changes, anticipating the other's response, time travel, pause, etc.) not afforded real-life interactors (Honeycutt, Zagacki, & Edwards, 1989). However, IIs should not be confused with fantasies. This distinction is discussed next.

Differences Between IIs and Fantasy

Fantasies are a type of respondent thought (Klinger, 1981). Previously, my colleagues and I attempted to distinguish IIs from fantasy (Honeycutt et al., 1989). Caughey (1984) discussed fantasy as a type of daydreaming in terms of a sequence of mental images that occur when attention drifts from focused rational thought. In contrast, IIs simulate conversational encounters that individuals expect to experience or have experienced during their lives. Some of these encounters may never transpire or may be quite different from what was envisioned. Yet communication fantasies involve highly improbable or even impossible communication encounters. Thus, talking with deceased others or celebrities are fantasies and rarely serve as the basis for real communication exchanges (Edwards et al., 1988). Indeed, previous studies of II partners reveal that many of the IIs occur with romantic partners (33%), friends (16%), family members (12%), individuals in authority (9.4%), work associates (8%), ex-relational partners (6%), and prospective partners (4%; Edwards et al., 1988; Honeycutt et al., 1989-1990; Zagacki et al., 1992).

MODES OF IMAGERY FOR IIS

Imagined interactions occur in different modes of imagery. Three primary modes of imagery are verbal, visual, and mixed. Clearly, individuals can think verbally about their discoursing—without forming mental images of the interactive scene, the other, or themselves.

Although the precise connection of verbal information to visual information in imagined interactions is unclear, it is plausible that information stored verbally serves a different function than information encoded visually. In fact, some support for the functional nature of mental images in relation to social action is provided by Lord (1979; see also Anderson, 1983). Lord demonstrated that individuals process information about the self in verbal or propositional form (e.g., "I am honest"), whereas information about others is interpreted and reconstructed by using visual images. This is because, Lord argued, information about others is more visually prominent to actors than information about the self. Moreover, actors must constantly interpret visual information about others while not having direct visual access to similar information as it relates to the self. In the latter case, actors rely on more verbally based data.

Aside from visual, verbal, and mixed imagery, two other imagery distinctions are worthwhile to make. There is the *omniscient perspective*, where individuals see themselves along with other interactors in conversations, much as individuals view themselves on videotape. Another point of view is the *direct perspective,* where individuals see only other interactors much as they would during real conversations. These distinctions are important because they provide cognitive researchers with information about the quality of individual representational systems. They also address the extent to which cognition about the external environment are verbally and/or visually mediated (see Lord, 1978). Kroll-Mensing (1992) found that individuals sometimes imagine a conversation involving two or more other people in which the individual is an observer. The imagined observation of other people consists of friends, family, acquaintances, and ex-significant others such as romantic partners.

Berger (1997) provided examples of the direct imagery mode in a series of planning studies in which individuals comprised plans for achieving particular types of social goals. The research revealed that individuals who were thinking of plans for asking someone for a date or planning for meeting a potential new roommate to get the other to like the self, recalled previous, specific episodes in similar situations in which they had done this. The role of the individual in the recalled, specific episodes was a central figure seeking to achieve the goal rather than as a detached observer of the scene.

A final imaging consideration concerns the distinction between immediate and reflective operations of IIs. Individuals are capable of shifting from the immediate mode in which they experience directly or omnisciently an II to a reflective mode where they move out of the II to deliberate over the happenings in the II and then move back into the immediate mode. This may be associated with rehearsal and message planning as contingency plans are envisioned. Singer (1985) indicated how thoughts may be modified and acted on by further thoughts in much the same way that experience is modified by new information from the environment. These further thoughts may be an instance of the reflective operation of IIs.

SUMMARY

IIs are derived from symbolic interactionism (Mead, 1934). They have characteristics similar to actual conversations such as being fragmentary, extended, rambling, repetitive, or coherent. Actors in imagined interactions may control conversations or relinquish control to others (Edwards et al., 1988). IIs frequently occur during the course of an actor's day. Through IIs, individuals can accurately represent many of the physical and socioemotional elements of real interaction. Our self-concepts are developed and manifested through IIs.

Daydreaming occurs with great frequency in everyday life. IIs are a type of daydreaming and occur in different time modes, including thoughts about the past, current events in our lives, and the future. Many of our daydreams are concerned with issues in our interpersonal relationships.

IIs occur in different imagery modes. We use visual, verbal, and mixed imagery in which we imagine the scene of the encounter as well as what we are saying. IIs may use a direct perspective, where we see the other person similar to what is envisioned in real conversations. However, IIs may also reflect an omniscient perspective similar to watching ourselves on videotape. We see ourselves talking to others in this type of imagery.

Chapter 2

CHARACTERISTICS

OF IIS

Honeycutt (1989) noted that IIs can serve as the means through which one is capable of testing or imagining the consequences of alternative messages prior to or after actual interaction. In early descriptions of how IIs work, Honeycutt compared them to cartoons, in which each panel represents the logical sequence of events as envisioned by an individual engaging in the use of IIs. IIs allow a person the luxury of moving back and forth over the panel, perhaps even rewriting the sequence if appropriate and necessary.

IIs were first proposed by Rosenblatt and Meyer (1986) as a tool used in clinical settings for allowing patients to visualize interaction with others who were not emotionally or physically available to them. IIs were seen as possessing many of the same characteristics as real conversations in that they may be fragmentary, extended, rambling, repetitive, or coherent. They proposed IIs as a means of problem solving by allowing an individual to think through a problem.

IIs operate as a mechanism to operationalize the study of intrapersonal communication as it works to shape communication interpersonally. In Honeycutt et al. (1989), we stated the following:

> The notion that intrapersonal communication involves "talking" to oneself is important, but somewhat limited. For, in our view, not only do individuals talk to themselves, but during imagined interactions they imagine themselves

13

talking to others as well. Thus, we surmise that IIs are an extended form of intrapersonal communication. (p. 168)

MEASURING IMAGINED INTERACTIONS

From the conception of IIs and their application to communicative encounters, researchers were faced with the same difficulty as other cognitive researchers in that measuring IIs must rely largely on the inferences based on external behavior (Honeycutt et al., 1989). Measuring mental states is a lofty and difficult task. Introspective self-report was recognized early on for its potential contribution to uncovering the dimensions and uses of IIs.

Honeycutt and his colleagues (1989) developed a two-part instrument that came to be called the Survey of Imagined Interactions (SII). Appendix 2.1 contains sample prototypical items. It is stressed that items may be added or deleted depending on the situation in which the survey is administered. The survey's introduction describes IIs as "those mental interactions we have with others who are not physically present" and follows with a description of some likely characteristics such as

> being ambiguous or detailed and how they may address a number of topics or examine one topic exclusively. The interactions may be one-sided where the person imagining the discussion does most of the talking, or they may be more interactive where both persons take an active part in the conversation. (Honeycutt, 1991).

Part I of the initial survey consisted of statements about IIs that required responses on a 7-point Likert scale ranging from *NO!* to *YES!* Aside from the verbal labels for the scale positions, the yes–no continuum provides an excellent visualization of the intensity of scale differences. Respondents have often revealed that they like the scale because of its visual imagery.

Various items measure the frequency or activity of having IIs as well as if they occur before or after conversations with others. Additional items measure how detailed and specific they are, who talks the most (self or other) in the interaction, the valence or pleasantness of the II, who they are with, how similar or discrepant they are from real conversations, and whether they can hear and see the other. Participants are also asked whether their IIs tend to involve visual, verbal, or mixed imagery. Open-ended items ask for a list of topics and interaction partners that they recall. Although the SII is easily administered to individuals in its present form, other researchers may choose to measure only selected features or functions rather than include them all depending on the samples of individuals under study. In addition, the SII may be modified for other contexts.

Part 2 asks participants to concentrate on their most recent II. Participants indicate whom it was with, when it took place, the scene of the II, and the topics under discussion. Item 43 asks individuals to write down a sample protocol of dialogue if possible. Some people are unable to report a protocol. However, the vast majority of respondents reports a few lines. Previous work has coded indexes of self-dominance in the sample protocols (Edwards et al., 1988; Honeycutt et al., 1989b; Zagacki et al., 1988). These indices includes who uttered the first and last lines (1 = *self*, 0 = *other*). The number of lines and words uttered by self and other is counted. In addition, earlier research has coded the success and emotional intensity in the II (Zagacki et al., 1988).

Coders evaluate how successful the II was for the respondent (1 = *high success*, 2 = *medium success*, 3 = *low success*). Emotional intensity has used a three category scheme: 1 = *strong emotion*, 2 = *moderate emotion*, 3 = *neutral emotion*. These have been cross-tabulated with II topics and dialogue partners. Respondents indicate whether they experienced or re-experienced the II as they wrote down the protocol and the feelings that accompanied it. They finally respond to items exploring the functions of the II and how much communication satisfaction they felt concerning the II.

EVIDENCE OF VALIDITY FOR SII DIMENSIONS

Confirmatory factor analysis has continued to support the dimensions of IIs that were originally identified in earlier studies (Honeycutt, Zagacki, & Edwards, 1992-1993). The SII has consistently demonstrated good construct validity (Nunnally, 1978). Honeycutt and his colleagues (1989) discussed how II data may also be gathered by oral interviews and journal accounts. A triangulation of these kinds of data-collection procedures has revealed that the SII responses are representative of II features and characteristics. Individuals easily relate to the concept and indicate they have them often.

Although the SII is easily administered to individuals in its present form, other researchers may choose to measure only selected features or functions rather than include them all depending on the samples of individuals under study (Honeycutt, 1989). In addition, the SII may be modified for other contexts (e.g., Honeycutt, 1999; Honeycutt & Wiemann, 1999; Zagacki et al., 1988). Versions of the SII have been tailored for specific populations of individuals including the elderly, marital/dating partners, debaters, and foreign individuals as well as assessing the correspondence between an II that occurred before a real encounter and the actual conversation.

There is evidence of convergent validity for the valence index. This index correlates with Hecht's (1978) communication satisfaction index ($r = .38$, $p < .001$, Zagacki et al., 1988). The general, self-dominance index correlates with the self speaking more words in the Sample II protocol ($r = .15$, $p < .01$) and negatively correlates with the other speaking more words ($r = -.13$, $p < .03$).

The representational validity of the classification of the coders' judgments in terms of reflecting kinds of emotional intensity and success is necessary to establish because communicators' reports of what they were thinking may be incongruent with a researcher-imposed interpretation of the meaning of the codes (Poole & Folger, 1981). There is evidence of representational validity of these codes. For example, Item 45, in which the respondents report on their own feelings during the II, is consistent with coders' estimate of the participants' emotional intensity (Zagacki et al., 1992). Coders' evaluation of respondents' success in the II is compatible with the respondents' self-evaluation of communication success.

There are eight characteristics of IIs discussed in this chapter: frequency, retroactivity, proactivity, variety, discrepancy, self-dominance, valence, and specificity. *Activity* also referred to as *frequency* is measured by an index and represents how often individuals report having IIs (e.g., "I have IIs all the time"). The index measuring *proactivity* (e.g., "Before important meetings, I frequently imagine them") represents IIs occurring before anticipated encounters. The index measuring *retroactivity* (e.g., "After I meet someone important, I imagine my conversations with him or her") assesses the occurrence of IIs after an encounter. The *variety* factor measures topic and partner diversity (e.g., "Most of my imagined interactions are with different people").

Discrepancy is an index measuring the incongruity between IIs and the actual interaction (e.g., "More often than not, what the other actually says in a real conversation is different from what I imagined he or she would say"). *Self-dominance* measures the extent to which an individual reports him or herself talking in IIs as opposed to the partners in the IIs (e.g., "When I have imagined interactions, the other person talks a lot"). The *valence* factor measures the degree of conflict or pleasantness of IIs (e.g., "My imagined interactions are usually quite pleasant"). *Specificity* measures the degree of detail as opposed to being vague or abstract (e.g., "When I have imagined interactions, they tend to be detailed and well-developed"). Box 2.1 is a summary of II characteristics and their relationship with selected communication variables.

FREQUENCY

Frequency refers to the frequency and regularity of having IIs. Women report more IIs than men (Edwards, Honeycutt, & Zagachi, 1989). Research assessing the association between the occurrence of IIs and an individual's level of loneliness has revealed a negative relationship between the two variables (Honeycutt, Edwards, & Zagacki, 1989-1990). Simply stated, those who are chronically lonely experience fewer IIs. They also suggest that those who report higher levels of II activity also report more self-dominance.

BOX 2.1

Summary of II Characteristics and Their Relationship to Selected Communication Variables

Comm. Variable	Frequency	Proactivity	Retroactivity	Variety	Discrepancy	Self-Dominance	Positive Valence	Specificity
Communication competence				—				
Detecting meanings			+					+
Conversational Memory			+				—	+
Conversational Alternatives				+				+
Perceiving Affinity		+						
Interpretation	+							
Conversational Dominance			+					
Eavesdropping Enjoyment					+			
Loneliness				—		+		—
Locus of Control			—	+				
Overall conversational Sensitivity			+	+				+

Note. —: negative relationship between the II characteristic and the communication variable. +: positive association between the II characteristic and the communication variable.

17

Increased use of IIs, or higher frequency, has been found to be associated with a decrease in discrepancy for individuals competing in debate tournaments (Gotcher & Honeycutt, 1989). Couples experiencing geographical separation from one another have reported that they experience an increase in the number of IIs when they are separated (Allen, 1994). Honeycutt and Wiemann (1999) reported that marital status is related to the use of IIs, in that engaged couples report having more IIs than do those who are married. As revealed in Box 2.1, frequency is positively associated with conversational interpretation. This is the ability to detect irony or sarcasm in what others say and being able to paraphrase what others have said (Daly, Vangelisti, & Daughton, 1987).

Kroll-Mensing (1992) found that anxiety and depression were positively related to the frequent occurrence of IIs. Anxiety was also associated with reporting that IIs clarify thoughts, relieve tension, and plan interpersonal goals. The presence of an increased frequency of IIs for anxious and depressed individuals makes sense in terms of the viewpoint that research suggests that the relationships of anxious and depressed individuals are characterized by conflict and dissatisfaction (e.g., Cane & Gotlib, 1985; Goldstein & Chambless, 1978). Their IIs may reflect the conflict that they are experiencing in their interpersonal relationships. Kroll-Mensing (1992) also found that approximately 75% of her participants reported having at least one II over a 3-day sampling period. In fact, on Day 1, 105 respondents reported 189 IIs; on Day 2, 88 respondents reported 146 IIs; on Day 3, 69 respondents reported 106 IIs.

However, Kroll-Mensing (1992) indicated that these figures may underestimate the frequency of IIs. The design of her study may have provided a disincentive to report the occurrence of IIs over the 3-day period because they were then asked to rate qualities about the IIs that comprised an additional 28 items to respond to everyday.

PROACTIVITY

It is important to note that IIs can have characteristics of being proactive or retroactive. *Proactivity* refers to those IIs that are engaged in prior to actual interaction, and research has shown that such IIs tend to occur prior to actual interactions rather than after (Zagacki et al., 1992). Research has suggested, for instance, that individuals who measure high in Machiavellianism experience more proactive IIs. Kroll-Mensing (1992) also found that reports of IIs appear to be future focused.

In research conducted to assess the use of IIs during competitive debate, proactive IIs were shown to be correlated with imagined success during competition rounds, but not with actual success (Gotcher & Honeycutt, 1989). The use of IIs appears to aid competitors in psychologically preparing for actual competition and may serve to create success through self-fulfilling prophecy (Honeycutt & Gotcher, 1991). More about the function of IIs in forensic competition is discussed in chapters 5 and 8.

Box 2.1 reveals that proactivity is positively associated with perceiving affinity. Daly and his associates (1987) defined this as a communication skill in sensing, liking, attraction, or affiliation between communicators. Proactivity is also positively correlated with loneliness (Honeycutt & Ford, 2001). This means that lonely individuals imagine conversations beforehand although they still have few IIs.

RETROACTIVITY

Retroactivity involves reviewing the interaction once it has taken place. For example, a worker may desire a raise, so he or she decides to approach the boss concerning the matter. Using an II proactively, he or she may imagine going into the boss' office and devise a plan for what may be said to the boss. Once the real-life interaction has taken place, perhaps the worker will reflect on the actual interaction, analyzing it to determine what worked and what did not. This is an example of making use of a retroactive II. Kroll-Mensing (1992) found that a majority of IIs was proactive (53%), whereas 30% were a replay of prior conversations.

Research suggests that conflict was associated with low satisfaction with IIs (Zagacki et al., 1992). Noting that at first glance this finding may appear inconsequential, the researchers proceeded to suggest this is not the case. They purported that the finding

indicates that at least some individuals do not use imagined interactions to think through their conflict toward more satisfactory conclusions by composing alternate message scenarios for future use, but instead review and rehearse the negative dimensions as a total experience. (p. 65).

This study (Zagacki et al., 1992) yielded results that suggest IIs associated with positive emotions occur less frequently and with lower levels of retroactivity than those with mixed emotions. The researchers noted the surprising nature of such findings, in that one might expect persons to dwell on pleasant communicative episodes to extend the benefit of positive feelings. However, the findings actually suggest that individuals do not engage in such II activity. Rather, once pleasant communicative experiences are acknowledged, they are simply taken for granted and not often recalled. Another possibility is that individuals avoid reviewing what they perceive to have been pleasant communicative episodes through the use of IIs for fear of finding potentially discrepant information that could possibly lead to an unpleasant state.

Retroactivity is correlated with proactivity (r = .34; Honeycutt et al., 1989-1990). Honeycutt (1995) also noted how many IIs are linked together to form themes of relationships. Although a retroactive II is experienced, it may be immediately linked with a proactive II (e.g., "Last time, I bit my lip. Next time, I see him or her, I am going to say exactly how I feel"). Given that IIs tend to occur with significant others, it may be that many of them are linked and occur between encounters reviewing and previewing conversations.

As revealed in Box 2.1, retroactivity is associated with a number of communication variables. It is positively correlated with detecting meanings, which is the tendency to sense the purposes and hidden meanings in what individuals are saying in conversations (Honeycutt et al., 1992-1993). It is associated with memory about conversations as individuals report a high level of recall for prior conversations. It is related to conversational dominance, which is a skill that determines who has power and control within conversations (Daly et al., 1987).

However, retroactivity is negative associated with an internal locus of control. An internal locus of control means that individuals believe they control their own destiny. An external locus of control reflects the belief that you are a victim of environment or circumstances that are out of your individual control (Rotter, 1975). This makes sense because retroactive IIs mean that conversations have already taken place and the person is replaying prior events. Unfortunately, proactivity was not positively associated with an internal locus of control (Honeycutt et al., 1989).

Retroactivity is positively associated with conversational sensitivity. This is a personality trait in which individuals are able to recognize the verbal and nonverbal messages, whereas others take conversations at face value and seldom wonder about the underlying relationships and meanings that are implicit in every conversation. It is associated with self-monitoring, empathy, self-esteem, social skills, assertiveness, lack of communication apprehension, and tendency to praise others (Daly et al., 1987).

VARIETY

Variety refers to the diversity of topics and partners within IIs. Some individuals imagine conversations with many people, whereas others tend to think about the same topics with the same people. Variety has been shown to be moderately correlated with II proactivity and retroactivity (Honeycutt et al., 1989-1990). IIs that involve a variety of people as well as different topics are related to the imaginer's internal locus of control (Honeycutt & Ford, 2001). This finding lends credence to the idea that the chronically lonely lack variety in their IIs. Research suggests that IIs involve a wide variety of topics, including conflict, dating, activities, school, and family/home and include various partners such as family members, dating partners, friends, and roommates (Edwards et al., 1988). In a subsequent study, Honeycutt, Zagacki, and Edwards (1989) found that college students had most of their IIs with romantic partners (33%), followed by friends (16%), family members (12%), authority figures (9.4%), coworkers (8%), ex-relational partners (6%), and prospective partners (4%). These data demonstrate that IIs involve significant others rather than strangers or acquaintances.

Kroll-Mensing (1992) obtained similar results. She found that friends were the most frequently reported interaction partner followed by acquaintances, family members, and ex-significant others. She also found that approximately one third of IIs occur with individuals with whom the respondents did not have a satisfactory relationship in real life. Conflict is kept alive and associated with anxiety. This is discussed in terms of the conflict management function in chapter 5.

As revealed in Box 2.1, variety is positively associated with conversational alternatives. This refers to flexibility in talking and being skilled at wording the same thought in a number of ways. Variety is negatively associated with loneliness, but positively associated with an internal locus of control and overall conversational sensitivity.

Variety is demonstrated in the following journal account from a 22-year-old female student who kept a journal for a week of the individuals she most thought about after being exposed to the characteristics of IIs in class lecture. She reported that most of her IIs were with her boyfriend, roommates, and family members. She also wrote:

> I found out some devastating news about my younger sister a few days ago and consequently I have had numerous IIs with her as well as my mother. My mother asked me to talk to my sister about it and I have been rehearsing and having retroactive IIs that have helped me figure out how to approach the topic. These IIs's have been very frequent.

DISCREPANCY

IIs can be similar to or different from relevant interaction. Discrepancy is the II characteristic that provides for the incongruity between IIs and the actual interaction that they address. Research suggests that individuals who are chronically lonely have been found to have highly discrepant IIs, which researchers suggest serves to perpetuate their lonely state (Edwards et al., 1988). Lonely people have limited prior interactions on which to base their IIs, so any IIs that they experience prior to new interaction are high in discrepancy. Discrepancy has been found to be negatively correlated with communication competence (Honeycutt et al., 1992). Furthermore, Kroll-Mensing (1992) found that depression was associated with discrepant IIs.

Box 2.2 contains a sample journal account that reflects discrepancy between an II and a real encounter.

BOX 2.2
Sample Journal Account of a Discrepant II

Last summer I met a girl in Florida and we wrote each other for quite some time. We both kept saying we wanted to see each other, but our plans never materialized. Finally, in September, she was going to fly to New Orleans to see me. From the moment she told she was coming to visit, I began imagining what it would be like when we saw each other. I figured we would embrace passionately at the airport and have a million things to say to each other. I figured we would go out Friday night to the French Quarter and go to bars. She had never been to a bar before. At the time, the drinking age was 18 in New Orleans and 21 in Alabama (her home state). Saturday I planned for us to go to the Riverwalk all day and then go out again that night. On Sunday morning, I was supposed to bring her to Biloxi where she had a ride home to Alabama.

Well, welcome to reality. When she got off the plane, we kind of half-hugged each other and really didn't know what to say to each other. Most of our conversation was small talk. After we got to my house and showered, we went to the French Quarter. We probably didn't stay there any longer than an hour before we decided that we were exhausted and ready to get some sleep. Surprisingly, Saturday was pretty much like I had planned. We spent the whole day at the Riverwalk and really enjoyed ourselves.

However, Saturday night was a different story. We began the night as I had planned by going to bars. Then the real excitement began. At about one o'clock in the morning she told me she had to make a phone call. After she got off the phone, I was informed that she had to leave for Biloxi right then. Instead of spending a nice evening out with her, I spent most of the night driving to Mississippi. This was definitely a good example of an imagined interaction being quite different than the actual experience. (Reprinted from Honeycutt, 1989)

According to Honeycutt and his associates (1992-1993), even if the II is discrepant from a real encounter, the process of rehearsing anticipated encounters enhances self-confidence because the individual can practice possible responses and dialogue. High discrepancy in the II comes from the participant's lack of skill in predicting likely results from the interaction partner. Discrepant IIs reflect an inability to plan effectively and imagine alternative outcomes (Allen & Honeycutt, 1997).

Research has also looked at the role of IIs as used by individuals preparing for competitive debate during forensic competition. Gotcher and Honeycutt's (1989) findings suggest that higher frequency of IIs decreases discrepancy, alluding to the increased ability to construct an imagined situation, which closely mirrors reality through the use of IIs (Honeycutt & Gotcher, 1991). This finding, the researchers noted, seems to relate to the self-fulfilling prophecy.

The relationship between the mode of imagery and its affects on discrepancy has been explored. Zagacki et al. (1992) discussed how verbally based IIs are usually less similar to the actual communication they represent. Thus, through a syllogistic approach, if conflictual IIs are more verbal and verbally based IIs are usually discrepant, then conflictual IIs are more discrepant and distort reality.

Box 2.1 shows that discrepancy is negatively associated with communication competence and positively associated with loneliness. In addition, it is correlated with eavesdropping enjoyment. This is the extent to which individuals enjoy listening to conversations.

SELF-DOMINANCE

IIs also include the characteristic of *self-dominance*. This addresses who is more prominent in the II, self or other. Early research suggests that self-dominance in the II was associated with having less pleasant IIs (Honeycutt et al., 1989-1990). Research also suggests that a person engaging in IIs who is concerned with matters of conflict will likely find the self is more dominant than the partner they imagine in the II. Typically, we see ourselves doing more of the talking while the interaction partner says less and is in more of a listening role (Edwards et al., 1988). Analysis of II protocol reveals more words and lines of dialogue uttered by the self in contrast to what the interaction partner is imagined to say. In addition, the self tends to start the conversation in the II (Zagacki et al., 1992). Again, the rehearsal function of IIs is an important consideration here. Recall that verbal imagery is associated with having conflictual IIs (Zagacki et al., 1992). The rehearsal function of IIs reflects self-dominance as attention is concentrated on one's messages.

Kroll-Mensing (1992) found that the self was the main speaker in a majority of IIs. Less popular were IIs in which the other person was the main speaker. It was common for there to be dialogue by self and interaction partner, yet the self still talks a little more.

VALENCE

Another II characteristic is a reflection of the degree of emotional affect produced while having an II. This is referred to as *valence* in terms of pleasantness. In

Honeycutt, Edwards, and Zagacki (1989-1990), we reported that females report more pleasant IIs. Those who reported less pleasantness in their IIs reported higher levels of self-dominance. Kroll-Mensing (1992) found that, for males, IIs were more helpful in resolving conflict, sharpening arguments, exploring causes of conflict, and devising ways of getting even with interactional partners. Males also spoke more in their IIs and were less satisfied with their interaction partner in real life. Kroll-Mensing (1992) suggested that IIs, similar to mental imagery in general, are experienced as positive and comfortable when they are characterized by the individual feeling in control of his or her situation rather than being a victim of outside forces beyond his or her control.

Research has suggested that more pleasant IIs elicit positive affect, whereas those that are less pleasant—often involving conflict—elicit negative affect. Honeycutt, Zagacki, and Edwards (1992) reported a finding that suggests that II pleasantness negatively predicts recall of conversations. Hence, the more pleasant the II, the less memory an individual has of it. This finding suggests that recalling past conflictual or unpleasant interactions is a means by which memory about conversations operates so that when a person is remembering an interaction, he or she may be going back and replaying a previous encounter that was unpleasant (Honeycutt et al., 1992). Thus, IIs accompanied by more negative affect are more memorable than more pleasant IIs. Perhaps this explains why negative information or IIs may be recalled more readily and have higher informational value than positive information or IIs.

Klinger (1987) discussed how we are more likely to react with emotion when we encounter a cue related to the pursuit of some goal. There is also evidence that imaginary experiences have effects on emotion similar to real experiences and that images are initiated through motivational as well as emotional processes like real behavior (Klinger, 1981). If this is the case, then IIs that serve a rehearsal function should be related to measures of emotional affect insofar as it can be argued that rehearsal is goal-directed and makes us attentive to the cues that may produce incongruity between desires and expectancies. Because IIs can be conceived as a planning activity containing corresponding intentions, IIs should be associated with emotional affect. We have found that pleasant emotions were associated with having more IIs that are similar to actual encounters (Honeycutt et al., 1989-1990).

In some thought-sampling research, the data have revealed that thoughts were concerned with the subject's present-life concerns 67% of the time and with past and future concerns 24% of the time. Thoughts about the past tended to involve reviewing previous events and using critical evaluation (Klinger, 1987). Thoughts about the future tended to be in the form of rehearsals and setting up alternative scenarios for anticipated events. According to Singer (1987), this "helps us to maximize the lessons we draw from past experiences and to plan better ways of dealing with upcoming contingencies" (p. 8).

Support for Klinger's (1987) notion of emotion being concerned with current concerns is reflected in some of our findings. For example, we had coders evaluate the level of emotional intensity (1 = *low intensity*, 2 = *medium*, 3 = *strong*) as well as having individuals responding to the SII report their own level of emotional affect after having recalled the most recent II (1 = *positive*, 2 = *neutral*, 3 = *mixed feelings*, 4 = *negative*) and the level of communication satisfaction they felt with the II (Zagacki et al., 1992).

Strong intensity was associated with low communication satisfaction, whereas medium intensity was associated with high communication satisfaction. Strong intensity was also associated with negative and mixed feelings, whereas medium intensity was associated with positive emotions. In addition, we found that highly intense IIs occurred with romantic partners and family members, with less intense IIs occurring with work partners. High intensity was associated with II topics dealing with relational conflict, whereas medium intensity was associated with topics related to school, work, and small talk (Zagacki et al., 1992).

We also had coder judgments of the success of the II (1 = *low success*, 2 = *moderate*, 3 = *high*). Highly intense IIs were associated with low success, whereas medium intensity associated with high success. In addition, individuals with positive feelings reported fewer IIs as well as having fewer retroactive IIs than individuals reporting mixed feelings. We have posited that individuals who experience retroactive IIs may go through a process of recasting the original experience with each successive II. Swann, Griffin, Predmore, and Gaines (1987) posited that cognitive responses reconstruct affective responses. IIs may play a role in this process. The II may allow the individual to project the perspective of the other while gaining additional information about the experience. This idea is consistent with findings by Tesser and Leone (1977), in which thinking about a person results in a polarized evaluation of the person. Thus, IIs may allow one to consider characteristics of another while strengthening emotions associated with the other.

Negative affect in IIs may be linked with Sherman and Corty's (1984) simulation heuristic. According to this heuristic, individuals who narrowly fail to achieve certain goals may find it easier to construct counterfactual scenarios that would have led to success. To the extent that retroactive IIs simulate earlier unsuccessful experiences, the individual may imagine the same encounters under more successful outcomes. Yet the reconstruction and construction of scenarios that avoid failure may evoke strong negative affect (Zagacki et al., 1992).

Research has been conducted examining the use of IIs in relation to Machiavellianism (Allen, 1990). Machiavellianism reflects the degree to which an individual is willing to manipulate others in interpersonal situations. Individuals measuring high in Machiavellianism were more likely to report IIs that were less pleasant than those low in Machiavellianism.

The mode of imagery is associated with the level of II pleasantness as well. Verbally based IIs are less pleasant (Zagacki et al., 1992). These less pleasant

IIs concern conflict and are usually more verbal, as opposed to visual, in nature. As revealed in Box 2.1, positive valence is negatively aligned with remembering conversations. Individuals may be more likely to recall arguments rather than positive encounters. There is research on initial impressions and the negativity effect in which negative impressions are remembered more than positive ones. More is said on the conflict-management function of IIs in chapters 3 and 5.

SPECIFICITY

Another II characteristic is *specificity,* which refers to the level of detail and distinction of images contained within IIs. In a study looking at couples' IIs use by virtue of attachment style, Honeycutt (1999a) found that those couples reporting a secure attachment style experience high levels of detailed visual and verbal imagery, suggesting high levels of specificity. He suggested that this level of specificity aids in greater recall of the IIs.

Honeycutt, Zagacki, and Edwards (1992-1993) conducted a study to assess the use of IIs and the correlation with communication competence as well as conversational sensitivity. Their results suggest that the level of detail in IIs, or specificity, positively predicts several dimensions of conversational sensitivity, including the ability to detect meanings in another's messages, conversational memory, conversational alternatives, and conversational memory (see Box 2.1).

Specificity is also negatively correlated with loneliness (Honeycutt et al., 1989). Hence, lonely individuals have vague IIs. They are not able to imagine lines of dialogue by the self or the interaction partner compared with less lonely individuals.

EXAMPLES OF II CHARACTERISTICS
FROM TWO INTERVIEWS

To demonstrate how the characteristics of IIs are manifested, a sample interview is presented in which two individuals' responses are compared. The interviewees were with two college students who were asked about their IIs. The students were 19 and 23 years old. They were asked what they were thinking about, frequency of daydreaming, topics of interaction, and with whom they often have IIs. Following are examples of the specific characteristics of IIs that were mentioned.

Proactivity. Both persons had IIs in which they anticipated what was going to be said next. Hence, they experienced proactive IIs.

Retroactivity. Both individuals had retroactive IIs. However, there was a difference between them. The older individual used retroactive IIs to be proactive in the future, whereas the younger individual used retroactive IIs to relive what had already taken place. This individual would be frustrated because these IIs provided no future outlet of action. Hence, the older individual had linked IIs in which prior conversations were replayed while preparing for ensuing encounters.

Frequency. The 19-year-old reported more IIs than the 23-year-old.

Self-Dominance and Discrepancy. The younger person reported talking more in her IIs as opposed to listening compared with the 23-year-old and also revealed a lack of control in real-life actions and situations. Hence, the IIs often involved imagining saying things that could not be said in real-life encounters.

Valence. The older person revealed that many IIs were positive in nature, whereas the younger person stated that there was negative and positive affect. However, the younger person wanted to reduce the number of negative IIs because they produced frustration.

Specificity. Both individuals had specific IIs. The older person used them to solve disputes with a romantic partner. She would imagine exact comments said by her and him. In contrast, the younger person described an II where a person appeared at the front door, and they talked about signing a petition for sewage drainage relief in the area.

Variety. Both interviewees reported that most of their IIs were with their romantic partners, friends, and family members, although the younger person mentioned someone wanting money.

SUMMARY

There are eight characteristics of IIs. Proactivity and retroactivity are concerned with the timing of the II in relation to actual conversations. Proactive IIs occur before an anticipated encounter, whereas retroactive IIs occur after the encounter. Proactive and retroactive IIs can occur simultaneously as individuals replay prior conversations in their minds while preparing for ensuing interactions. Other characteristics of IIs are frequency, in that individuals vary in how often they imagine conversations and valence in which persons have positive, negative, or mixed feelings while imagining conversations. Individuals vary in how discrepant their IIs are from real encounters. Lonely individuals have fewer IIs (low frequency), but when they have them, their IIs are higher in discrepancy. The variety characteristic of IIs reflects individual differences in the number of topics discussed in the IIs and whom they are with. IIs tend to occur with significant others such as relational partners, family, and friends. They do not occur with people whom we rarely see.

IIs are used for message planning. Hence, most of the imagined talk comes from the self, with less emphasis being placed on what the interaction partner says. This reflects the self-dominance characteristic. The final characteristic of IIs is specificity. Individuals vary in the extent that they recall specific lines of dialogue said by self or the interaction partner. Specific IIs also occur through visual imagery as individuals imagine the scene of the II (e.g., office, bedroom).

APPENDIX 2.1:
SURVEY OF IMAGINED INTERACTION (SII)

Imagined interactions (IIs) are mental interactions we have with others who are not physically present. People may have imagined conversations that occur in self-controlled daydreams or while the mind wanders. Sometimes they may occur after a real interaction has taken place. IIs may be brief or long. They may be ambiguous or detailed. They may address a number of topics or examine one topic exclusively. The interactions may be one sided, where the person imagining the discussion does most of the talking, or they may be more interactive, where both persons take an active part in the conversation. With your help, we can better understand the functions of IIs. Thank you very much for your participation.

ID No: _____   Date: _____   Sex: M F   Age: _____

Following are a few items asking you about your experiences with imagined interactions with others. Please read each item carefully and try to answer it as honestly as possible.

YES! = very strong agreement   NO! = very strong disagreement

YES = strong agreement   NO = strong disagreement

yes = agreement   no = disagreement

                    ? = neither agreement or disagreement

1.   I have IIs many times throughout the week.

               NO! NO no ? yes YES YES!

2.   I often have imagined interactions *before* interacting with someone of importance.

               NO! NO no ? yes YES YES!

3. Most of my imagined interactions are with different people.

   <u>NO</u>! NO no ? yes YES <u>YES</u>!

4. I often have imagined interactions after interacting with someone of importance.

   <u>NO</u>! NO no ? yes YES <u>YES</u>!

5. When I have imagined interactions, they tend to be detailed and well developed.

   <u>NO</u>! NO no ? yes YES <u>YES</u>!

6. I have recurrent imagined interactions with the same individual.

   <u>NO</u>! NO no ? yes YES <u>YES</u>!

7. In my real conversations, I am very different than in my imagined ones.

   <u>NO</u>! NO no ? yes YES <u>YES</u>!

8. After important meetings, I frequently imagine them.

   <u>NO</u>! NO no ? yes YES <u>YES</u>!

*9. Most of my imagined interactions are with the same person.

   <u>NO</u>! NO no ? yes YES <u>YES</u>!

*10. I usually say in real life what I imagined I would.

   <u>NO</u>! NO no ? yes YES <u>YES</u>!

11. My imagined interactions usually involve conflicts or arguments.

   <u>NO</u>! NO no ? yes YES <u>YES</u>!

*12. When I have imagined interactions, the other person talks a lot.

   <u>NO</u>! NO no ? yes YES <u>YES</u>!

13. I frequently have imagined interactions.

   <u>NO</u>! NO no ? yes YES <u>YES</u>!

*14. I do not enjoy most of my imagined interactions.

   <u>NO</u>! NO no ? yes YES <u>YES</u>!

15. When I have a real conversation that I have imagined, the actual conversation is very different from what imagined.

   <u>NO</u>! NO no ? yes YES <u>YES</u>!

16. After I meet someone important, I imagine my conversation with them.

   <u>NO</u>! NO no ? yes YES <u>YES</u>!

*17. I rarely imagine myself interacting with someone else.

   <u>NO</u>! NO no ? yes YES <u>YES</u>!

18. In my real conversations, other people are very different than in my imagined ones.

    <u>NO</u>! NO no ? yes YES <u>YES</u>!

*19. My imagined interactions are quite similar to the real conversations that follow them.

    <u>NO</u>! NO no ? yes YES <u>YES</u>!

20. I enjoy most of my imagined interactions.

    <u>NO</u>! NO no ? yes YES <u>YES</u>!

*21. It is hard recalling the details of imagined interactions.

    <u>NO</u>! NO no ? yes YES <u>YES</u>!

22. My imagined interactions are very specific.

    <u>NO</u>! NO no ? yes YES <u>YES</u>!

*23. My imagined interactions are usually quite unpleasant.

    <u>NO</u>! NO no ? yes YES <u>YES</u>!

24. I talk a lot in my imagined interactions.

    <u>NO</u>! NO no ? yes YES <u>YES</u>!

*25. The other person has a lot to say in my imagined interactions.

    <u>NO</u>! NO no ? yes YES <u>YES</u>!

26. My imagined interactions are usually enjoyable.

    <u>NO</u>! NO no ? yes YES <u>YES</u>!

*27. The other person dominates the conversation in my imagined interactions.

    <u>NO</u>! NO no ? yes YES <u>YES</u>!

28. My imagined interactions usually involve happy or fun activities.

    <u>NO</u>! NO no ? yes YES <u>YES</u>!

29. Before important meetings, I frequently imagine them.

    <u>NO</u>! NO no ? yes YES <u>YES</u>!

30. I have imagined interactions with many different people.

    <u>NO</u>! NO no ? yes YES <u>YES</u>!

31. I dominate the conversation in my imagined interactions.

    <u>NO</u>! NO no ? yes YES <u>YES</u>!

32. In my imagined interactions, I can "hear" what the other person says.

    <u>NO</u>! NO no ? yes YES <u>YES</u>!

33. Before I meet someone important, I imagine a conversation with them.

      <u>NO</u>!   NO   no   ?   yes   YES   <u>YES</u>!

34. More often than not, what I actually say to a person in a real conversation is different from what I imagined I would say.

      <u>NO</u>!   NO   no   ?   yes   YES   <u>YES</u>!

35. More often than not, what the other actually says in a real conversation is different from what I imagined he or she would say.

      <u>NO</u>!   NO   no   ?   yes   YES   <u>YES</u>!

*36. When I have an imagined interaction, I often only have a vague idea of what the other says.

      <u>NO</u>!   NO   no   ?   yes   YES   <u>YES</u>!

37. My imagined interactions tend to be on a lot of different topics.

      <u>NO</u>!   NO   no   ?   yes   YES   <u>YES</u>!

38. During my imagined interactions, I tend to see and concentrate attention on:

      Myself __:__:__:__:__:__:__   Other person
                 Both

39. My imagined interactions are:

___mostly verbal (e.g., they involve talking with little visual imagery)

___mostly visual (e.g., little talking occurs)

___are a mixture of verbal and visual

40. List some of the topics you recall discussing in some of your most recent imagined interactions.

41. Please indicate with whom you have most of your imagined interactions (e.g., romantic partner, sister, etc.).

42. Please describe the most recent imagined interaction you had. Be sure to indicate your relationship to the person, how long ago it took place, where you imagined the interaction, where the actual interaction scene took place, and what topic or topics were discussed.

    a.   Relationship with other_____

    b.   How long ago it took place_____

    c.   Please describe the scene of the imagined interaction (e.g., it takes place in an office, apartment, it took place nowhere in particular).

    d.   Topic or topics discussed:

43. Please write down some sample lines of dialogue said by each speaker in your imagined interaction such as you might find in a play script. This will help us identify who said what. (Use the back of this sheet if necessary.)

44. I reexperienced this imagined interaction as I was writing it down

        ____No   ____Yes

45. My feelings during this imagined interaction were:

        _____mostly positive _____neutral

        _____mostly negative _____a mixture of positive & negative

46. The imagined interaction I just reported helped me to actually talk about feelings or problems later with the interaction partner.

        NO! NO no ? yes YES YES!

47. The imagined interaction helped me understand my partner better.

        NO! NO no ? yes YES YES!

48. The imagined interaction helped me understand myself better.

        NO! NO no ? yes YES YES!

49. The imagined interaction helped me in clarifying my thoughts and feelings with the interaction partner.

    NO! NO no ? yes YES YES!

50. The imagined interaction helped me plan what I was going to say for an anticipated encounter.

    NO! NO no ? yes YES YES!

51. I had the imagined interaction before entering a situation with someone whom I knew would be evaluating me.

    NO! NO no ? yes YES YES!

52. The imagined interaction helped me relieve tension and stress.

    NO! NO no ? yes YES YES!

53. The imagined interaction made me feel more confident when I thought I was going to actually talk with the interaction partner.

    NO! NO no ? yes YES YES!

54. I had the imagined interaction to practice what I was actually going to say to the person.

    NO! NO no ? yes YES YES!

55. The imagined interaction helped me to reduce uncertainty about the other's actions and behaviors.

    NO! NO no ? yes YES YES!

56. The imagined interaction I just reported was a very enjoyable conversation.

    NO! NO no ? yes YES YES!

57. I was very satisfied with the conversation.

    NO! NO no ? yes YES YES!

58. I enjoyed the conversation.

    NO! NO no ? yes YES YES!

59. I relieve old arguments in my mind.

    NO! NO no ? yes YES YES!

60. It is sometimes hard to forget old arguments.

    NO! NO no ? yes YES YES!

61. Imagining talking to someone substitutes for the absence of real communication.

    NO! NO no ? yes YES YES!

62. I use imagined interactions to think about someone with whom I have a close bond.

NO! NO no ? yes YES YES!

63. Imagined interactions help keep relationships alive.

NO! NO no ? yes YES YES!

64. I often cannot get negative imagined interactions "out of mind" when I'm angry.

NO! NO no ? yes YES YES!

65. Imagined interactions can be used to substitute for real conversations with a person.

NO! NO no ? yes YES YES!

66. Imagined interactions sometimes help me manage conflict.

NO! NO no ? yes YES YES!

67. By thinking about important conversations, it helps relieve tension or stress.

NO! NO no ? yes YES YES!

68. Imagined interactions may be used to compensate for the lack of real, face-to-face communication.

NO! NO no ? yes YES YES!

69. Imagined interactions are important in thinking about one's relational partner.

NO! NO no ? yes YES YES!

THANK YOU FOR PARTICIPATING IN THIS INTRIGUING SURVEY!!

Scoring the SII Dimensions

Characteristics of IIs. Items with an asterisk (*) have to be reverse coded using the following scale: 1 = 7, 2 = 6, 3 = 5, 5 = 3, 6 = 2, 7 = 1. The 4 stays unchanged. Previous factor-analytic research of Section 1 has revealed eight dimensions that reflect general characteristics of IIs (Honeycutt et al., 1992-1993). The first factor represents the discrepancy between imagined and real interactions ($\alpha = .84$). The dimension contains seven items (Items 7, 10*, 15*, 18, 19*, 34, 35). The second dimension contains five items and reflects valence or the pleasantness of the II ($\alpha = .85$; Items 14*, 20, 23*, 26, 28). The third factor contains four items and reflects activity or how often an individual reports having them ($\alpha = .76$; Items 1, 6, 13, 17*). Self-dominance is the fourth factor and represents how much one perceives the self-talking relative to the other (α = .77; Items 12*, 24, 25*, 27*, 31). The fifth factor is specificity, which reflects how detailed the IIs tend to be (α = .73; Items 5, 21*, 22, 32, 36*). Retroactivity is the sixth factor in which IIs occur after important encounters (α = .80; Items 4, 8, 16).

The seventh factor is variety, which represents having IIs on a variety of topics and with different people (α = .67; Items 3, 9*, 30, 37). The eighth factor is proactivity, where IIs occur before important meetings (α = .73; Items 2, 29, 33).

Items 40 and 42d concern II topics. Previously, these have been coded into topics of conflict/relational problems, dating, work/job, school, recreation/activities, family/home, money, friends/roommate relationships, ex-partners/ex-friends, and small talk (Edwards et al., 1988; Zagacki et al., 1992). Items 41 and 42a reflect the relationship of the respondent with whom many of the IIs are with as well as in the most recent one.

This includes such categories as relational partners (e.g., spouse, boy/girlfriend), prospective partners (casual acquaintances), family members, friends, work associates, roommates, people in authority, enemies/hostile relationships, and ex-partners (Honeycutt et al., 1989; Zagacki et al., 1992). Item 42b, reflecting how long ago the most recent II took place, has previously been coded: 1 = *within same day,* 2 = *yesterday,* 3 = *within previous week,* 4 = *1–2 weeks,* 5 = *over 2 weeks ago.* Many individuals report having the II within the previous week or less (Zagacki et al., 1992).

Item 42c reflects the scene or location of the II. The following codes have been used: 1 = *my room/home,* 2 = *other's room/home,* 3 = *in bed,* 4 = *on the phone,* 5 = *public place,* 6 = *office or work setting,* 7 = *car,* 8 = *miscellaneous.*

Item 43 asks for the sample lines of dialogue. Some people are unable to report a protocol. However, the vast majority (74.5%) reports a few lines. Previous work has coded indexes of self-dominance in the sample protocols (Edwards et al., 1988; Honeycutt et al., 1989; Zagacki et al., 1992). This includes who uttered the first and last lines (1 = *self,* 0 = *other*). The number of lines and words uttered by self and other is counted. In addition, earlier research has coded the success and emotional intensity in the II. For example, coders may evaluate how successful the II was for the respondent (1 = *high success,* 2 = *medium success,* 3 = *low success*). Emotional intensity has used a three-category scheme: 1 = *strong emotion,* 2 = *moderate emotion,* 3 = *neutral emotion.* These have been crosstabulated with II topics and dialogue partners.

Functions of II. It is important to note that the function items on this sample survey reflect measuring three functions for the most recent II (Items 46–58). The self-understanding factor is reflected by four items (α = .70; Items 46–49). The second function is "rehearsal" for an anticipated encounter (α = .75; Items 50, 51, 53, 54), whereas the third factor reflects catharsis or releasing tension (α = .61; Items 52, 55, 67). Items 56–58 come from Hecht's (1978) Communication Satisfaction Inventory (α = .89) and have been reworded to reflect an II.

Items 59 to 69 reflect measuring three other functions in terms of reports of their general IIs. However, it is critical to note that the researcher can modify these items to reflect the most recent II as was done for the self-understanding, rehearsal, and catharsis functions. Conversely, those items (Items 46–58) and requisite functions could be modified to measure IIs in general if the researcher desired that.

Conflict management is reflected by the following items: 59, 60, 64, 66 (α = .81). Compensating for the lack of communication is scored by adding items 61, 65, and 68 (α = .73). Maintaining relationships or keeping them alive in one's mind are reflected by the following items: 62, 63, 69 (α = .70). The SII can always be modified to raise internal consistency for some of the factors. Again depending on the researcher's needs, items may be added or deleted depending on which characteristics and functions are important. The functions may be measured in terms of overall or general IIs as well as in specific contexts or the most recent II.

Chapter 3

FUNCTIONS

OF IIS

The preceding chapter identified eight characteristics of IIs. However, six functions of IIs have been identified. A functional approach to the study of IIs identifies the purposes that this type of mental imagery and daydreaming serves in everyday life. The six functions are: (a) they keep a relationship alive, (b) thinking about or resolving conflict, (c) they are used to rehearse anticipated interactions, (d) they aid an individual in self-understanding in terms of clarifying thoughts and feelings, (e) they serve as a form of catharsis by relieving tension and reducing uncertainty, and (f) they serve to compensate for the lack of real communication (Honeycutt, 1991).

MAINTAINING RELATIONSHIPS

In terms of keeping relationships alive, earlier research surrounding imagined interactions sought to uncover their role in impacting interpersonal communication. Honeycutt, Zagacki, and Edwards (1989) suggested that often the most important determinants of relational development occur outside of immediate conversation in the cognitive realm that includes imagined interactions. While examining the relationship between the person having the II and his or her II partner, studies have indicated that 33% are with romantic partners, 16% are with friends, 12% are with family members, 9.4% are with individuals in authority, 8% are with people from work, 6% are with ex-relational partners, and 4% are with prospective partners (Honeycutt et al., 1989). From those data it has been determined that IIs are predominated by thoughts of significant others rather than with strangers or acquaintances.

Duck (1980) suggested that explorations of relational communication should involve interpersonal research that looks at interpersonal relationships as they evolve outside of direct relational encounters in terms of processes such as replaying relational events during time spent alone, planning future encounters, and remembering the pleasures of encounters. The study of imagined interactions has provided for a means of investigating such phenomena (Honeycutt, 1989). "IIs can psychologically maintain relationships by concentrating thought on relational scenes and partners" (Honeycutt, 1995, p. 143).

Recent research has investigated the use of IIs by geographically separated couples as a means of maintaining the relationship (Allen, 1994). Stating that the II research program has established the relational significance and serves specific purposes for anticipated relational encounters, Allen designed a study to explore II usage in relieving tension caused by separation. Sampling 40 couples, half of whom were in geographically separated relationships, Allen used a revised version of the SII to make her assessments. Indications are that couples who are geographically separated experience increases in the number of IIs during times of separation and view their use as a coping strategy. This would seem to suggest that IIs are tools that allow individuals to continue their relationships when circumstances prevent actual interaction. The study's findings also suggest that relational couples geographically separated experience increased understanding as a result of their II usage, as well as greater use of IIs for rehearsal. Together these findings suggest that IIs can and do serve a significant role in perpetuating relationships.

Although imagined interactions may create a relationship, they also shape it as it goes through certain stages of development. The memory structure approach to IIs suggests that not only do IIs bring the relationship into existence, they can also serve to shape the developmental progression of said relationship (Honeycutt, 1995). The assumption of such an approach is that individuals have certain expectancies in terms of the developmental stages of relationships that can be used in the formulation of an expected prototype for categorizing another's as well as one's own relationship. As new observations of relationships are made, they are assimilated into the expectancies and revisited in the form of IIs. These IIs may serve to keep an existing relationship intact, or maybe to rehearse for the initiation of a new one. In these terms, IIs enable the process of thinking about a relationship even through its various developmental phases.

The memory structure approach assumes that individuals have particular expectancies for the development of interpersonal relationships (Honeycutt & Cantrill, 2001). Some of these expectancies are more mindful as opposed to being mindless in terms of not being given much thought. Expectancies for relational development can be used as an anchor prototype for categorizing the type of relationship observed between others as well as one's own relationships (Honeycutt & Cantrill, 2001). Relationship expectancies may be reinforced as observed behavior is assimilated into existing categories (e.g., self-disclosure). Occasionally, accommodation takes place in which the expectancies are modified to account for new observed behavior. For example, a faithful partner loses trustworthiness after being discovered for infidelity. Regardless if assimilation or accommodation takes place, the person may play over in his or her mind, images of conversations with their relational partner. These imagined interactions might relive previous encounters and link these to anticipated conversations. The imagined interactions might serve a function of keeping relationships intact, rehearsing for the ending of relationships as well as the initiation of relationships such as planning to ask someone for a date (Berger & Bell, 1988). The function of imagined interaction in keeping conflict alive in personal relationships is discussed in the next section.

CONFLICT MANAGEMENT AND RESOLUTION

Keeping the relationship alive has a downside, in that conflict within a relationship can also be kept alive as well as reduced. In his discussion of the retroactivity and proactivity characteristics of IIs, Honeycutt (1991) noted that IIs may occur before or after actual encounters, with these characteristics not necessarily being mutually exclusive. Thus, he indicated that some IIs may have simultaneous features such that they occur after an encounter and previous to the next. This idea suggests that IIs can link one interpersonal episode, including conflict, to the next. Research in various areas has served to support this idea of IIs linking interaction.

In research examining the role of humor in marital relationships, Honeycutt and Brown (1999) suggested this interconnection between the retroactive and proactive roles of IIs by linking it to the telling of jokes. Proactively, a spouse, they suggest, may rehearse a joke for the purpose of telling it to the other spouse. The spouses may then interact, at which time the joke is shared. The joke teller may then experience retroactive IIs for the purpose of reviewing the positive and/or negative responses of this spouse. "This retroactive II may lead the person to further rehearse the joke hoping to improve delivery, decide to never try the joke again, or think of another person that may appreciate the joke" (Honeycutt & Brown, 1999, p. 4). Thus, the spouse can rehearse or replay a past joke-telling interaction mentally for the purpose of becoming better prepared for the next interaction that may involve the telling of the joke.

In his article addressing the oral history interview as a means of studying marital couples and their use of imagined interactions, Honeycutt (1995) reported discussion of questions concerning IIs and conflict resolution during the interview. Memories of conflict, re-experienced as retroactive IIs, are acknowledged by couples as keeping conflict alive. However, some couples report that the IIs can serve as a mechanism for dealing with suppressed conflict that is not being discussed openly. Honeycutt reported that using the oral history interview in the study of marital couples has revealed that spouses often report imagining conversations with their partner concerning a number of topics when not in the other's presence. The oral history interview is a semistructured narrative that allows married couples to reconstruct events from the relationship's past. The interview also includes discussion of how the couple met, what attracted them to one another, philosophy of marriage, problems in the marriage, and so on. Spouses' imagined conversations include the issue of conflict, where one may replay an encounter involving conflict and regret not having said various things currently in one's mind. This replaying involves the use of retroactive IIs, with proactive IIs being used to rehearse for the next encounter with the spouse, such that the conflict picks up where it was left. He noted that when discussing this notion during the oral history interview, "couples eagerly relate to the concept and provide examples of imagining conflict in their minds with their partner over some issue" (Honeycutt, 1995, p. 66).

The retroactivity and proactivity aspects of imagined interaction can work simultaneously to link one interaction to the next with a specific interaction partner (Honeycutt, 1991). Thus, if Person X and Person Y experience conflictual interaction characterized by conflict, Person X may reflect on the conflict making use of imagined interaction's dimension of retroactivity. Person X may re-experience the negative affect associated with the original conflict and use this reflection as a means of envisioning exactly what is said to Person Y during the next interaction between X and Y. It is possible that the retroactive II that occurs as a product of the initial conflict acts as a preinteraction stimulus for the next encounter with that partner (Honeycutt, 1995).

Although the linking of prior and anticipated encounters occurs in both positive (e.g., relationship maintenance for geographically separated couples) and negative (e.g., conflict maintenance) situations, research suggests that the more common occurrence includes conflict. Zagacki et al. (1992) reported that the most common case of reported IIs involves thinking about conflict. In an attempt to assess the role of emotion and mental imagery on the use of IIs, they asked respondents to complete the SII, including both the closed- and open-ended responses. On the open-ended section of the survey, one item that participants were asked to describe related to the topics they discussed in their imagined interactions (see Item 42d in Appendix 2.1). The topics were coded into 1 of 11 categories based on the following themes: conflicts/problems, dating, school/class, work/job, activities, family, money, friends, ex-partners, small talk, and miscellaneous. The topic most reported involved conflict, with those of dating, family, and friends following. With such a high occurrence of IIs involving conflict, it seems that much cognitive effort and time is invested in dealing with such topics.

A recent study conducted by Johnson and Roloff (1998) was conducted as a means of assessing factors contributing to the problem of constant arguing in relationships and its effects on relationship quality. In examining the factors that affect resolvability of a given conflict, they found that perceived resolvability was negatively associated with the following items: (a) arguments arising from violated expectations, (b) countercomplaining and partner-initiated demand–withdrawal, (c) predictability of argumentative episodes, (d) overall discord, (e) withdrawal after a conflict episode, and (f) mulling over the argument. The relevant factor from this study in relation to conflict-linkage is the last item—mulling. Mulling, which includes mentally reliving the argument over and over, seems to be related to the use of retroactive IIs, which allow an individual to revisit an episode once it has taken place. According to conflict-linkage theory, the revisiting of conflict may also be accompanied by the reformulation of points and counterpoints for future interaction (Honeycutt, 1991, 1995). Thus, IIs can help link unresolved or a series of conflict episodes together.

Chapter 5 discusses the conflict management and the resolution function of IIs in more detail. II conflict-linkage theory is presented based on a series of axioms and corollaries designed to explain the nature of conflict and resolving conflict in everyday life.

REHEARSAL

IIs have been shown to aid in the planning process to help reduce anxiety and increase speech fluency (Allen & Honeycutt, 1997). In this study, an experiment was developed to investigate the effects of the independent variables of a planning task and discrepant IIs on the dependent variable of anxiety as operationalized through the use of object adapters. The participants completed the SII and then participated in the experimental part of the study that involved videotaping. In this portion of the study, participants were asked to devise a plan for convincing a friend with a drinking problem to seek help. One group of the participants was placed in a distracter-task condition to minimize their message-planning time. The other group was given time solely to rehearse their plan for convincing a friend to seek help for the drinking problem. Both groups then engaged in the role-playing activity with a friend. These role-playing tasks were videotaped and assessed for frequency of object adapter use by participants. Results of the study indicate that individuals who were able to plan their conversations displayed fewer object adapters than those who completed the distracter task (Allen & Honeycutt, 1997).

Geographically separated couples (GSCs) have been found to make particular use of IIs for the purpose of rehearsing future interactions (Allen, 1994). In comparison with couples who are not geographically separated, GSCs reported greater use of imagined interactions for the purpose of preparing for the next interaction with their partners. Such a result seems to suggest that GSCs emphasize an efficiency meta-goal that is in operation during times of separation.

Rehearsal help us make decisions. When we face a difficult decision, we may be paralyzed in moving forward. Rather, we are immobilized by uncertainty over projected outcomes. IIs may help us explore the rewards and costs of choosing one course of action over another. Klinger (1990) reviewed studies involving a group of women who were asked to pick a difficult decision that they had been thinking about and to indicate how committed they were to the course of action they would most likely choose.

The women faced various decisions, such as whether to break up with a boyfriend, switch their field of study in college, and where to go for an upcoming vacation. A control group of women performed some arithmetic problems and went home. Two other groups spent time in controlled daydreaming. One group imagined with great specificity the positive benefits of one of the courses of action they had been thinking about such as leaving their boyfriend. The second group imagined in detail the things they would say to carry out the course of action. Just before they left the research session, the groups indicated again how committed they were to the decision they had made in their mental imagery. Three weeks later, they received a survey asking how they currently felt about their decision.

The women who had earlier made the most committed decisions were those who had imagined in detail the things they would say and do to implement the decision. Furthermore, those who earlier had imagined only the positive benefits that result from their decision instead of thinking about how to implement the decision felt more committed to the course of action right after the session, but 3 weeks later they had become uncertain about their course of action. The group who had done the arithmetic problems was further away from a decision 3 weeks later than they had been at the beginning. Klinger (1990) concluded that if you wish to make a decision, you might benefit from daydreaming in detail what you would do to carry it out. Klinger is also isolating the positive benefits of the specificity characteristic of imagined interactions discussed in the previous chapter.

Wilensky (1983) discussed how "planning includes assessing a situation, deciding what goals to pursue, creating plans to secure these goals, and executing plans" (p. 5). Plans are broader than IIs because rehearsal is just one function. Plans may be nonverbal in the pursuit of actions or goals (e.g., realizing it is your anniversary coming up and buying a gift that does not involve any communication). When used for rehearsal, IIs allow for a decrease in the number of silent pauses and shorter speech onset latencies during actual encounters and allow for an increase in message strategy variety (Allen & Edwards, 1991).

Finally, rehearsal has been analyzed in relation to attachment styles. Regression analysis revealed that a secure attachment is predicted by rehearsal as compared with other attachment types (Honeycutt et al., 1998-1999). This is discussed in more detail in chapter 4, which specifically examines the relationship maintenance function of IIs. Perhaps strategic planning for various encounters may enhance security in romantic relationships. This use of IIs also seems to be linked to cognitive editing, which allows adjustments to messages after their potential effects on a given relationship have been assessed (Meyer, 1997). The implication is that individuals rehearse messages, presumably through the use of IIs, and make changes as necessary for achieving desired outcomes.

SELF-UNDERSTANDING

Rosenblatt and Meyer's (1986) original conception of II for use in therapy recognized that II, which involves explaining or relating things to another, aids in the self-clarification process. IIs may help uncover opposing or differing aspects of the self. Klinger (1990) also discussed more generally how daydreaming facilitates self-understanding. It reflects desires as well as what is feared even if we would rather not know.

Research assessing the use of IIs by GSCs suggests that they experience IIs as a tool for increasing self-understanding more than do couples not geographically separated (Allen, 1994). The results seem to suggest that GSCs have a greater need to develop better understanding prior to interaction because of the limitation on interaction time due to their geographic circumstances. The use of IIs helped create a better understanding of the partner as well as the self. Allen (1994) suggested that GSCs may also use IIs to discuss certain issues with the relational partner so as not to be forced to deal with the given issue that may have been deemed unimportant during precious and limited interaction time.

Zagacki et al. (1992) studied the role of mental imagery and emotion in IIs and found that IIs, which involved more conflict, were related to an increase in self-understanding. IIs that provided increased self-understanding were also found to involve more verbal imagery, with the self playing a greater role in the II or being more dominant.

Pregnant women who talk to their unborn fetus provide another example of self-understanding. Stainton (1985) interviewed first- and second-time pregnant mothers about their emotions and feelings while carrying a child. First-time mothers reported talking to their unborn baby more when they were alone—a privilege not afforded to the expectant father. In addition, mothers also imagined talking with their unborn child when in the bathtub, while dressing, and while driving their cars to and from work. A number of mothers actually talked to the growing fetus in the form of a monologue. However, other mothers described a type of inner-talk in the form of IIs, in which they experienced thoughts and feelings that were communicated to the fetus without words and that they felt their fetus listened to them in a state of quiet alertness. Stainton (1985) also reported that second-time mothers who imagined talk with their first-born child were doing so in the second pregnancy, whereas other mothers did not talk to their fetus during either pregnancy. Apparently, there may be a maternal style or personality trait associated with talking to the fetus.

Mothers typically imagined asking the fetus about their unborn baby's health as well as explaining about growth in their imagined interaction with their unborn babies. Furthermore, they imagined bargaining with the fetus reminding it that they had eaten properly and exercised, expecting an easy labor in return. Interestingly, fathers tended to ask the fetus to behave during labor and "to hurry out so they could see each other" (Stainton, 1985, p. 323).

CATHARSIS

Imagined interactions have been recognized for their ability to relieve tension and reduce uncertainty about another's actions (Honeycutt, 1989). Rosenblatt and Meyer (1986) proposed IIs as a means of emotional catharsis in counseling sessions, having found that IIs served as an outlet for their patients to release unresolved tension. Patients noted feeling less relational tension after having experienced IIs.

The catharsis function of IIs also may reflect transferring feelings to someone who is not the source or cause of the feelings. The transference phenomenon is known in the psychoanalytic literature for expression of emotions at a target that is not physically present. Freud (1958) observed intense passions in daily sessions with patients in which the patients transferred to the therapist childhood wishes, fantasies, and expectancies, although the therapist was trying to be objective and neutral. Patients would transfer their projections onto the analyst. Transference is pervasive in many human interactions to the extent that individuals bring hidden agendas to their interactions. Steiner (1976) argued that the transference phenomenon allows individuals to put the target of the transferred feelings in an empathic frame of mind permitting the individual doing the transference to feel understood. IIs used for catharsis reflect transference in common, everyday experience.

Allen and Berkos (1998) noted that individuals use IIs as a means of "getting things off their chest" when they know that certain behaviors or the expression of certain emotions is inappropriate in actual interactions. The use of IIs has also been associated with a reduction in anxiety level (Allen &

Honeycutt, 1997). When planning for an interaction, making use of IIs results in a lower occurrence of object adapters. This seems to suggest that when one uses IIs, reducing anxiety may be experienced. This seems to suggest that IIs help one release certain emotions in the form of catharsis. Honeycutt (1991) provided numerous accounts of individuals reporting how their IIs made them feel better and release anxiety.

Stainton's (1985) interviews with expectant mothers about their fetus represent the catharsis function of IIs. The mothers who imagine talking with their fetus and inquire about its health and bargain for a smooth delivery feel positive and an emotional release. A good example of catharsis is provided by a mother who reported that when she imagined talking with her fetus that the baby seemed to be much closer and she felt better.

An example of the cathartic function is from a 25-year-old female college student who kept a journal of her IIs for the past few days. She reported that many of her IIs were used to relieve frustration such as after she had an argument with someone. She used IIs to feel better about her position.

COMPENSATION

Another function of IIs is that they can serve to compensate for the lack of interaction. There is research that supports IIs' function for compensating for the lack of real interaction. From the beginning of development, IIs have been purported to serve in the place of real interaction when it is not possible (Rosenblatt & Meyer, 1986). In their discussion of IIs used for therapeutic purposes, they indicate that an individual may choose to use IIs in place of actually confronting a loved one in fear that the loved one would be hurt by the message.

Honeycutt (1989b) discussed the use of IIs as a means of compensation by the elderly who may not see their loved ones as often as they would like. He found that elderly individuals who lived in a retirement center had some IIs with children. They tended to have more IIs with children who visited regularly compared with children who rarely visited.

There is the stereotype of old, elderly parents ruminating about children who did not keep in contact. Indeed, we tend to have IIs with people we see in everyday life as opposed to those we rarely see. The prevailing tendency was to have IIs with friends and other residents at the retirement center. They did not spend a lot of time thinking about children who did not come to visit. Instead, they had IIs with a newly created social family.

The research focusing on geographically separated individuals and their increased use of IIs during separation for the purposes of coping is additional indirect support for the notion that IIs are used in the place of real interaction. An example of the compensation function comes from a student who kept an II journal for a few days for a class assignment. She wrote:

I don't get see my boyfriend as much as I would like because of school and work. Most of my IIs are about things that we have done in the past as well as what I see us doing in the future. I've even imagined the wedding ceremony vows. I've also imagined how happy we would be on that stressful and busy day.

Another student compensated for her lack of real conversation with her father. She reported that she often thought of sitting and talking with her father about what is going on in her life. She also wrote, "Through IIs, I reacquaint myself with him and attempt to have the perfect father-daughter relationship that we never had. Through my compensatory IIs, I not only get to have a relationship with my father, I get to have a good relationship with him."

SUMMARY

IIs serve six functions. A given II may simultaneously serve multiple functions. IIs maintain relationships, provide catharsis, create a better sense of self-understanding, and allow for rehearsal of anticipated encounters. They provide a level of compensation for the lack of real interaction and may substitute for interaction. IIs keep conflict alive and help individuals manage conflict as individuals relive conflict in their minds while anticipating future arguments. Indeed, the old maxim that "sticks and stones can break my bones but names can't hurt me" may be fallacious. Indeed, memories of old arguments may be enduring.

Chapter 4

KEEPING RELATIONSHIPS ALIVE
THROUGH IIs:
ABSENCE MAKES THE HEART
GROW FONDER

A critical function of IIs is the maintenance of relationships. Honeycutt and Cantrill (2001) discussed how the communication is the relationship. Yet when partners are not together, they may daydream about each other and imagine conversations with them. Fisher (1994) discussed a stage of relational development called *infatuation* in which another individual takes on special meaning. It may be an old friend viewed in a new light or a stranger. Characteristics of infatuation include intrusive thinking, in which many individuals report spending from 85% to 100% of their time thinking about their partner. Negative traits of the beloved are overlooked, whereas positive traits are aggrandized. Many emotions are felt including elation, hope, apprehension, uncertainty, shyness, fear of rejection, helplessness, irrationality, uncontrollability, unplanned or spontaneous actions, and longing for reciprocity. Box 4.1 contains a journal account of a woman imagining seeing a lover who has been away. Her account reflects the rehearsal and relationship maintenance function of IIs.

BOX 4.1
Maintaining A Relationship Through IIs

Andy and I both have had numerous imagined interactions concerning our relationship. An imagined interaction is a process that helps people in the construction of social reality. A person may develop visual or verbal scripts in their head to help him or her deal with certain situations. Imagined interactions serve specific functions: rehearsal for actual upcoming communication situations, evaluation after an important encounter, obtaining a greater sense of our own feelings, and improving our own self-knowledge. Perhaps the best example of imagined interactions being used in Andy's and my relationship occurred during our separation last summer.

It was a very difficult time for both of us because we missed each other so much. The thing that helped each of us deal with the pain was the use of imagined interactions. I was amazed to discover that we both had imagined interactions about the moment that we would be reunited at the end of the summer. Whenever I was feeling lonely or especially missing Andy, I would think about the moment we would be able to see each other again. I would imagine the inevitable embrace, kiss, and words of love that we would give to each other. I would rehearse over and over again in my head the things that I would tell Andy at that moment. Things like "I love you more than anything else in the world." At the actual moment, we did hug, kiss, and give romantic proclamations of love to one another, but then there was an awkward moment of silence for two reasons. First, we had each gone over in our head that moment so many times that we neglected to think about what would come next. Second, we were still in shock that we had finally been reunited. Now we both laugh when we think of that moment because we realize how rehearsed the whole thing was on both of our parts. Nevertheless, imagining conversations with each other and being together again helped us survive the separation. Through the process, we also learned a lot about how we felt about each other.

The role of perceptions in our relationship exposes probably our biggest weakness. We have had arguments over the time we've known each other simply because one or the other of us misunderstood what the other was trying to convey in a given statement. For example, once I became upset because Andy said, "I need some time alone" to me. I perceived the statement as meaning, "I want to break from this relationship for awhile." I discovered after a teary, accusatory argument that what Andy really meant was that he needed to study because he had some tests.

Imagined interactions create relational expectancies and contribute to our memories about relationships. Expectancies for relationships can be envisioned in the form of memory structures for relationships (Honeycutt & Cantrill, 2001). Memory structures for relationships help us make sense of behaviors that we observe in others' relationships and our own relationships, and they provide a sense of trajectory about where relationships are going or remain cast in some type such as a long-term friendship or a platonic, casual friendship.

Following is a discussion of common topics in interpersonal relationships that individuals often imagine discussing. Yet the act of thinking about the topics means that the interaction partner is the focus of our attention.

EMPIRICAL STUDIES ON II TOPICS ABOUT RELATIONAL CONCERNS

Recall from chapter 2 the variety of IIs in which individuals have IIs involving different interaction partners and topics. Eleven topics of IIs were found in a survey of college students by Edwards et al. (1988). These topics were arranged in descending order of frequency: dating, conflicts/problems, work, activities, school, miscellaneous (idiosyncratic topics), friends, family/home, money, small talk, and ex-partners.

A sample of 48 married couples was surveyed; they were asked to write down their topics of IIs for the past week. A coding system was used based on Honeycutt's (1989) Survey of Marital Issues index, which lists a variety of topics that couples commonly deal with in their relationship such as managing finances, relations with in-laws, job satisfaction, and so on. Box 4.2 lists the top 10 topics in descending order as well as husband and wife differences in the rank ordering.

BOX 4.2
Rank Order of Spousal II Topics

Topics	Combined Rank Order	Spousal Differences	
		Husband	Wife
Future plans	1	1	2
Sex life	2*	2	4
How we communicate	2*	6*	1
How we manage our finances	4	3*	4
Social life	5*	6*	3
Our relationship	5*	3*	6
Children	7*	6*	8*
Job	7*	5	10
Feelings/emotions	7*	9*	6
Fantasies	10	9*	8*

Note. *Denotes ties.

Dating was the most common topic of IIs among college students from the Edwards et al. (1988) study. However, among married couples, future plans and goals was the main topic for the husbands, whereas communication concerns was the most imagined topic for the wives. Edwards and her associates (1988) found that among college students, conflicts were the second most imagined topic. Yet the second topic most discussed by husbands and wives was a tie between sex life and communication. As revealed in Box 4.2, sex was the second most imagined topic for husbands, whereas it was fourth for wives. Interestingly, communication was the main topic for wives, whereas it was sixth for husbands. This finding is consistent with other research reported by Honeycutt and Cantrill (2001), in which women think more about communication in their personal relationships while men think about it less often. In reconciling the differences between the Edwards et al. (1988) findings and the married couples' reports of II topics, it is possible that some married couples are concerned with the enduring quality of their sex lives and communication, which if not taken care of can cause conflicts. Among dating couples, such problems may be ignored while the couples are in a state of bliss. Furthermore, the research by Fisher (1994) reveals that *limerence* is a temporary state of courtship consisting of passionate love, thinking about the partner while out of his or her physical presence, and having generally positive thoughts about the partner while ignoring negative thoughts about him or her.

An example of limerence comes from a student of mine who interviewed a man about his IIs during the past week. The interviewee was a man who discussed how his most recent II concerned a woman he had met at a charity event. He remembered the interaction that took place retroactively. Yet he was also having proactive IIs as he imagined what he would say to the woman the next time he encountered her.

BICULTURAL DIFFERENCES AMONG II TOPICS
BETWEEN AMERICAN AND BRITISH COUPLES

I have surveyed American and British couples about their II topics. We sampled 69 couples distributed evenly between Great Britain and the United States. American couples were most satisfied with the following topics: sexual compatibility, shared goals/interests, amount of time that your partner listens to you, partner's fidelity, how we communicate, how children are raised, and discussion of daily events.

In contrast, British couples were more satisfied with the following topics: partner's treatment of drugs/alcohol, household duties, management of finances, time spent together, how we fight, how parents or in-laws are treated, how affection is expressed, and satisfaction with sexual intercourse. In addition, Americans reported having more IIs as well as having IIs that were used for the rehearsal function. Furthermore, American IIs were characterized by more self-dominance in which they talked more in their IIs than their partners. However, American's IIs were more discrepant compared with British IIs, whereas the British IIs were higher in pleasantness as well as being used to keeping conflict alive.

These differences are interesting in terms of the United States and Great Britain sharing English as a common language. Frith and Wesson (1991) discussed how the similarity between America and Great Britain in terms of a common language, equal proportional rates of urbanization, industrialization, and political stability masks differences in terms of ideological and communication differences. They discuss how Americans are direct in their speech, whereas indirectness characterizes interpersonal and institutional communication in Great Britain. If this is true, then our finding that Americans talk more in their IIs than the British as well as simply having more IIs is compatible with Frith and Wesson's speculation. Direct speech may be a consequence of the internal planning of messages.

Lipset (1963) described the British as deferential and class-conscious, whereas the Americans were stereotyped as egalitarian and distrustful of authority. If we assume these stereotypes as a premise for bicultural differences among British and Americans, then it can be argued that the American culture has traditionally emphasized individual autonomy such as the instillation of the American dream concept, in which children are more successful than their parents. It is possible that the Americans reported more satisfaction on a variety of communicative issues because these issues have been negotiated within the relationship. The British emphasis on deference may result in repressed acceptance or indifference to communicative issues that have been assumed rather than negotiated within close personal relationships such as marriage. This interpretation is compatible with the perception of Americans being more outgoing and extraverted as opposed to the stereotype of British stoicism.

IIS AMONG DIFFERENT TYPES OF COUPLES

Honeycutt and Wiemann (1999) studied the correspondence between II characteristics and beliefs about talk among engaged and married couples. They surveyed 255 individuals who ranged in age from 18 to 72 years. Beliefs about talk reflects the idea that communication serves a number of strategic functions in daily encounters, such as providing information, reinforcing known information (e.g., repetition of statements), providing entertainment, providing attention, persuasion, signaling intimacy, and concealing information (Patterson, 1983). Patterson (1987) discussed two additional functions. The affect management function reflects the expression of emotion through controlling negative affect (e.g., masking anger) or maximizing positive affect through the expression of joy. Finally, there is a presentational function, in which an identity is communicated to others between relational partners through tie signs such as the wearing of similar clothing.

Honeycutt and Wiemann (1999) also distinguished married couples using Fitzpatrick's (1988) marital typology into Traditionals, Independents, and Separates. Traditionals have conventional beliefs about marriage such as emphasizing stability, sharing a lot of activities, and arguing over serious topics. Independents have a moderate amount of sharing, willingly engage in conflict over numerous topics, and endorse more contemporary ideologies about marriage such as believing that marriage should not hinder an individual's autonomy in any way.

Separates emphasize autonomy and are nonexpressive. They do not share a sense of togetherness. Separates are physically and psychologically differentiated. Separates endorse some traditional beliefs. They are conventional in marital issues, but support the values of individual freedom upheld by independents. Supporting two opposing values causes Separates to be ambivalent about their relational values. They may hold one value in a public setting while believing another value privately. Separates are not interdependent and report little expressivity in their communication. The separates have been described as emotionally divorced due to the lack of sharing.

In their study, Honeycutt and Wiemann found no Separates. However, they found that Independents talked more about communication, emotions, and arguing than Traditionals. These topics may be points of contention for Independents, whereas they are moot for Traditionals. The choice of topics for Independents may reflect the negotiation of rules for maintaining the marriage. Previously, Honeycutt and his associates (1992-1993) found that Independents were less likely to endorse a variety of rules for resolving conflict such as signaling positive understanding, rationality, being concise, and being considerate.

The importance of intrapersonal communication is demonstrated through these findings as the functions of talk are linked with specific characteristics of imagined interactions. Honeycutt and Wiemann (1999) found an association between a function of talk that involved enjoying serious discussion of issues, talking about events in the day, equality of talk, and having frequent, pleasant, and nondiscrepant IIs with the marital partner. In his marital interaction research program, Gottman (1994) discussed how talking about events in the day reveals differences between couple types. The discussion of daily events was related to meta-talk or talk about communication and talk about love.

Honeycutt and Wiemann (1999) also found that relational happiness was associated with being engaged and having pleasant IIs. This finding is important in terms of social cognition because it reveals that a common outcome of close relationships, relationship happiness, is reflected in the minds of individuals internally in the form of intrapersonal communication in which individuals imagine pleasant interactions with relational partners.

Engaged couples had more IIs that were used to compensate for the absence of their partner compared with married couples. However, married couples were more likely to use IIs to rehearse anticipated encounters with their partners than engaged couples. These findings can be interpreted in terms of the old maxim, absence makes the heart grow fonder. There may be less rehearsal among the engaged partners due to less conflict in the honeymoon phase of their relational development. In the next chapter, I discuss the conflict-linkage function of IIs in which conflict is kept alive in the absence of actual interaction.

Traditionals reported discrepant IIs that were used less for rehearsing of messages for anticipated encounters compared with Independents. Because little rehearsing is taking place, there could be more discrepant conversational outcomes from what was expected in an II. In a discrepant II, an imagined message is not communicated during an actual encounter. Traditionals may imagine encounters with their partners in which they are rehearsing messages that inhibit misinterpretation, misunderstanding, or confusion, resulting in active conflict. Traditionals engage in arguing and conflictual encounters less than independents. Fitzpatrick (1988) reviewed research indicating how traditionals tend to avoid conflict except over serious issues, whereas independents are more likely to disagree over a variety of topics.

ORAL HISTORY STORYTELLING AND IIS

Oral history interviews with couples are a powerful communication tool to examine marital satisfaction. The re-creation of past events forecasts the future. *Oral histories* are formally defined as "the collecting of any individual's spoken memories of his/her life, of people he or she has known, and events he or she has witnessed or participated in" (Romberger, 1986, p. 344). The oral historian is attempting to discover knowledge about the couple's history and interpretation of those experiences from the stories that are told. Gottman (1994) described the use of oral history interviews for married couples as a clinical tool indicative of behaviors that predict marital quality and divorce.

Within the interview, individuals describe how they met, what attracted them to each other, problems in the marriage, philosophy about marriage, and how their marriage compares to happy and unhappy marriages of friends. Honeycutt (1995a) discussed how IIs in the oral history interview are often event-oriented, imagining talk about some event about which the partner needs to be informed.

Honeycutt (1999b) examined IIs during an oral history interview in which they were again classified as Traditionals, Independents, or Separates. In addition, he also examined Mixed types. Mixed types occur when one spouse endorses a different orientation from his or her partner. The major Mixed type in the early research was a Separate husband and Traditional wife. Subsequent research revealed that no particular Mixed type predominated over others (Fitzpatrick, 1988).

Both husbands' and wives' marital happiness was predicted by pleasant IIs. In addition, Separates were less likely to imagine positive encounters and more likely to imagine speaking more to their partners in their IIs as opposed to listening to their partners compared with the other marital types. Fitzpatrick (1988) reported that Separates have low levels of companionship and sharing while valuing autonomy in terms of their use of space. They have been found to discuss separate identities, roles, activities, habits, and personalities.

An interesting profile of the Separates emerges. Their internal dialogues are less pleasant with their partner than Traditional and Independents. Gottman (1994) speculated that Separates who avoid conflict live with the pain of unsolved, solvable problems. He discussed how negative emotions are frightening for Separates and that Separates do not have the communication skills to work out unavoidable conflict. This is further discussed in the next chapter on keeping conflict alive.

REHEARSING JOKES IN MARRIAGE

IIs are used to rehearse jokes that are told with a spouse. Honeycutt and Brown (1998) investigated rehearsal and humor orientation in marriage. Individuals who are high in humor orientation value and express humor as they tell more jokes and laugh more than those lower in humor orientation (Wanzer, Booth-Butterfield, & Booth-Butterfield, 1994). They enjoy laughter and jokes as well as not taking events too seriously. Individuals high in humor orientation are commonly perceived as having a sense of humor. Humor orientation is associated with positive outcomes such as optimism and well-being (Wanzer et al., 1994).

Several researchers have studied the use of inside jokes and idioms in marriage (e.g., Honeycutt & Brown, 1998; Wanzer et al., 1994). Inside jokes are words, phrases, and sounds that evoke humor known only to members of the relationship. This creates a feeling of shared meaning and cohesiveness. Ziv and Gadish (1989) reported that this "secret language" or private jokes understood only by the partners "strengthened feelings of belonging and intracouple cohesiveness" (p. 760).

The production of humor may be associated with the rehearsal of jokes. The rehearsal function of IIs is relevant to humor orientation as individuals imagine telling a joke and anticipate various reactions to the joke. The planning of a joke often represents a pleasurable proactive II. A proactive II occurs before an anticipated encounter such as rehearsing how jokes might be said. A retroactive II occurs after the joke-telling episode when the person replays the joke and recalls positive or negative responses from his or her partner. This retroactive II may lead the person to further rehearse the joke hoping to improve delivery, decide to never try the joke again, or think of another person that may appreciate the joke. The communicator can rehearse or replay a joke-telling interaction mentally.

Honeycutt and Brown (1998) found that there was a positive association between humor orientation and using IIs to rehearse jokes. Additionally, husbands scored higher in humor orientation with their wives compared with their wives. Crawford (1989) showed that wives tend to laugh at their husbands' jokes to signal affiliation. Yet to allow a joke to realize its full impact, the joke-teller must rehearse the joke. This joke rehearsal must take the joke and move it from the unconscious realm of "oh that is a funny joke" to the more conscious realm of "how did that punch line work so I can tell my husband." IIs are a form of operant thought, not respondent thought as noted in chapter 1. Moving joke rehearsal from the level of unconscious thought to actively, mindfully rehearsing jokes may increase one's humor orientation.

ASSOCIATIONS BETWEEN II CHARACTERISTICS AND ATTACHMENT STYLES

Bowlby (1979) argued that people develop internal schemata of self and others that persist throughout life. The quality of relationships during childhood affects expectancies about love later in life. Carnelley and Janoff-Bulman (1992) found that different attachment styles were best predicted by the nature of the relationship with the mother as opposed to the father, quality of parents' marriage, number of times that individuals reported being in love, and number of times someone had been in love without the other person feeling the same way. Optimism about the success of future love relationships was predicted by the number of times an individual had been in love and the absence of unreciprocated love. However, optimism about having a successful marriage was predicted by the quality of the parents' marriage.

Carnelley and Janoff-Bulman (1992) also found that an anxious/ambivalent attachment was negatively associated with optimism about future love relationships and marriage. Anxious/Ambivalent types are characterized by obsession, jealousy, having emotional extremes, having an intense sexual attraction for another, and desiring a strong bond (Ainsworth, Blehar, Waters, & Wall, 1978). Anxious/Ambivalents report having overprotective mothers compared with the other attachments (Carnelley & Janoff-Bulman, 1992). Anxious/Ambivalents are preoccupied with having close relationships and are associated with a dominating style of conflict resolution as opposed to compromise or integration of arguments (Ainsworth et al., 1978).

Secure attachments represent the ideal expectancy that others will be loving and responsive. This attachment is related to having an accepting mother (Carnelley & Janoff-Bulman, 1992). Love is experienced as happy, friendly, and trusting. In describing their current romantic partners, secure attachments report more unqualified closeness compared with Avoidants and less dependence and commitment compared with Anxious/Ambivalents. Feeney and Noller (1991) concluded that secure individuals emphasized the importance of openness and closeness while seeking to retain individual identity.

Avoidant attachments report cold and rejecting mothers as well as a fear of intimacy under threatening conditions (Carnelley & Janoff-Bulman, 1992; Hazan & Shaver, 1987). Research reveals that Avoidants described current romantic partners in terms of limiting dependence, closeness, and affection in the relationship compared with Anxious/Ambivalents (Feeney & Noller, 1991). Conversely, Anxious/Ambivalents reported more unqualified affection compared with Secures and Avoidants.

Attachment researchers vary in the number of styles that are used to classify bonding. Hazan and Shaver (1987) used the tripartite classification based on two dimensions of closeness and anxiety. Bartholomew (1990, 1993) used a quadruple scheme in which Avoidants are divided into two types. Fearful Avoidants have a negative self-concept and doubt that others will be available. Dismissive Avoidants have a positive self-concept while disregarding others. They value independence and self-reliance rather than sharing. Latty-Mann and Davis' (1996) scheme consists of secure, preoccupied, avoidant, and ambivalent types.

Hazan and Shaver (1987) argued that there are two dimensions of attachment despite differences in factor-analytic rotation methods or the number of styles (three or four). Sanford (1997) found support for Hazan and Shaver's two-dimensional factor model rather than a three- or unidimensional model. These researchers found that closeness and anxiety characterized the two-dimension model.

Honeycutt (1999a) examined the correspondence between attachment styles and IIs. Attachment theory presumes that individuals construct internal models of early relationships that guide social behavior throughout life (Bowlby, 1979). Given that attachment styles and the mental models underlying them are developed and maintained through social interaction with others, IIs would help individuals maintain their attachment styles (Honeycutt, 1999a). For example, Anxious/Ambivalents might imagine that their relationships are deintensifying, that their partners are no longer interested in them, and that their lives will be miserable without the partner more often than do Secures or Avoidants.

Honeycutt (1999a) found that two of the attachment styles were predicted by II characteristics reflecting discrepancy, serving a rehearsal function, and having specific images of conversation. Individuals who have a secure attachment rehearse dialogue with partners, and what is imagined often comes to past in real encounters (low discrepancy). Furthermore, a secure attachment is associated with specificity. This finding means that Secures imagine conversations that are detailed in visual and verbal imagery. Individuals are able to recall the scene of IIs and lines of dialogue used by self or other (Honeycutt, 1989a).

These predictors of a secure attachment point to covert dialogues playing a role in keeping the secure style alive within the mind. In contrast, discrepant IIs corresponded with the Anxious/Ambivalents. Anxious attachments imagine relational encounters and then find that the actual interaction is different from what was constructed in the mind. It is possible that ambivalence evolves after a series of discrepant encounters. The individual wishes to be prepared, but learns that planning for encounters is to no avail.

Whereas imagining conversations may enhance secure attachments, cognition about conversation may not help the Anxious/Ambivalents. This interpretation is compatible with prior research in which Anxious/Ambivalents have more state and trait loneliness followed by Avoidants and Secures (Hazan & Shaver, 1987). In addition, Edwards and her colleagues (1988) found that loneliness was associated with having fewer IIs that are discrepant. Recall from chapter 2 that IIs are more of a hindrance for lonely individuals. Similarly, IIs do not facilitate relational encounters for Anxious/Ambivalents.

Although IIs may not enhance actual encounters for Anxious/Ambivalents because they are discrepant from real interactions, we also found that there were no II predictors of an avoidant attachment. By definition, Avoidants have few close attachments. Yet, previous research on partners of IIs reveals that they tend to take place with significant others including intimate relationship partners, friends, and family members (Edwards et al., 1988). Because Avoidants would have fewer attachments to think about, the characteristics of their IIs are not related in a systematic way to their avoidance.

USING IIS TO MAINTAIN LONG-DISTANCE RELATIONSHIPS

Long-distance relationships consist of intimates who are living apart and separated by geography. There are over a million couples in the United States who have long-distance relationships, and the numbers continue to rise due to dual careers, job location, and advancement. Many relational partners have satisfying jobs and little desire to give up their job and follow each other.

Stephen (1984) examined symbolic interdependence in terms of couples constructing a joint construction of reality and communication. Long-distance couples tended to experience higher levels of symbolic interdependence and optimism than couples living together. Long-distance couples talked about fewer topics during their phone conversations than intact couples. Indeed, the costs of long-distance calling may mitigate against long speaking times covering a variety of topics. Yet IIs may be used to compensate for the lack of shared time as well as being used to psychologically maintain the relationship.

Allen (1990) surveyed 40 couples ranging in age from 25 to 48. Half of the sample consisted of long-distance couples and the other half was in a nongeographically separated relationship. She found that long-distance couples had more IIs to increase self- and partner understanding as well as using IIs to rehearse phone messages. She speculated that because long-distance couples have less actual conversations, they use IIs to resolve relational issues in their mind. Allen also found that long-distance couples reported that their IIs were used as a coping strategy to maintain the relationship. In addition, the long-distance couples reported that they had more IIs during times of separation.

For these couples, "absence made the heart grow fonder" instead of "out of sight, out of mind." Regarding IIs being used by long-distance couples to increase self- and partner understanding, it may be that a number of imagined topics are not seen as being important enough to discuss during long-distance phone conversations.

An example of the compensation function of IIs being used to maintain a long-distance relationship comes from two former female students who kept a journal of their IIs for a period of 1 month. Box 4.3 contains sample excerpts.

BOX 4.3

Keeping A Long-Distance Relationship Alive Through IIs

Scenario 1: Studying in Europe—The student discusses how she met a man while studying in Europe for 3 months and that she had an intimate relationship with him for 2 months. He returned to the United States a week before she did. From the minute he left, she imagined encounters about the time that they would spend together.

I kept picturing what it was going to be like when we saw each other again in a new setting. I imagined us having tons of fun and having long conversations just like we did when we were overseas. It turns out that my positive imagined encounters were very similar to what actually happened when we saw each other again. However, since we live 5 hours apart and have busy schedules, we have only been able to see each other once since we've been back. This long-distance relationship has caused me to keep having IIs with him which so far has kept the relationship alive, as well as exciting due to the positive emotions I have about the relational initiation and growth. In other words, my positive interactions that go on in my head help the relationship survive, it helps me to keep the pleasant memories fresh in my mind, and it makes me look forward to the next time we can spend time together.

Scenario 2: Separated in Hawaii & California—This student discusses her separation from her boyfriend when he was in Hawaii and she was in California.

After Kevin left for the summer, I had many IIs about our relationship and the next time I would see him. It was hard being apart for the summer after spending our first 9 months together on a daily basis. What helped me get through each was day was the use of IIs. We both would imagine laying together in bed and talking about our futures. We used to do that before we were separated. Throughout the summer, I had spent so much time thinking about Kevin and psyching myself up for his return that it helped me stay close to him, though we were apart. Actually, I felt an incredible bond and even closer than I had when he was with me. Instead of feeling totally disconnected with him, IIs helped me get through the summer and look forward to our next encounter when he arrives from Hawaii.

IIS OF PARENTS WITH COLLEGE-BOUND STUDENTS

One of the most stressful events in life is the departure of a young adult going to college. The launching stage is one stage of the family life cycle in which children leave the parental home for military service, college, employment, or to form a new home or new families. During the launching stage, the needs of departing children may clash with the needs of parents to serve as role models, guiding elders, or conversation partners. If parents successfully achieve the launching of young adults, the relationship may become more balanced. Yet there may be stress accompanied from role transformation, ambiguity, or changing role expectations (Galvin & Brommel, 1986; Hoffman, 1988).

In an attempt to reduce anxiety, parents may develop coping strategies that enable them to contain the distress and to preserve their relationship with their departing children (Spierer, 1981). Successful coping strategies include the following elements: (a) developing expectations for progress, (b) rehearsing behavior, (c) testing behavior, (d) evaluating behavior, and (e) attempting multiple strategies. Although testing behavior and attempting multiple strategies may be accomplished during actual conversations, IIs enable launching parents to examine expectations, rehearse behaviors, speculate on the effectiveness of options, and devise multiple strategies.

If parents and college-bound students experience IIs in the launching stage, it is important to know whether IIs help parents and young adults cope. Woods and Edwards (1990) examined the IIs of parents and their children who were going away to college. They surveyed 72 parent–student pairs by giving a modified version of the Survey of Imagined Interaction (SII; Honeycutt et al., 1992-1993). This was the first child to go to college for 61% of the parents. The SII was administered to parents and incoming freshmen at pre-enrollment counseling sessions at Louisiana State University.

Box 4.4 lists the most common topics for parents and students. All of the topics concerned the college-bound student; none concerned the family as a whole. Many of the topics overlapped such as course of study, choice of college, living arrangements, and finances. However, students also reported IIs about independent living and social life, whereas parents were concerned with assuming responsibility and adjusting to college life.

BOX 4.4
II Topics of Parents and Students at Freshman Orientation

Rank Order by Parents	*Rank Order by Students*
1. Adjustment to college life (21%)	Housing arrangements (19%)
2. Assuming responsibility (18%)	Study habits/grades (16%)
3. Course of study (14%)	Social life (14%)
4. Finances (11%)	Finances (12%)
5. Study habits/grades (11%)	Course of study (9%)
6. Choice of college (9%)	Choice of college (7%)

Note. Numbers in parentheses reflect the percentages of parents and students mentioning the topic.

These subtle differences are important because they reflect the role orientation of the parents and their college-bound children. The focus of the parents seems to be the process, whereas the focus of the students appeared to be the being. Whereas students were looking at the destination (being a college student, independent living, social life), parents were sensitive to the journey (assuming responsibility, adjusting to college life). Parents also took a more holistic approach, with concerns ranging from hygiene to balancing academic and social life, whereas students were less aware of the range of issues associated with independent living and college life. Although both parents and their college-bound children experienced IIs during the launching stage, they appeared to be more important for the parents. Parents had them more frequently, invested with more emotion, and used them for rehearsal compared with their children.

Although the launching stage may create anxiety for parents, they reported more pleasant and positive emotions in their IIs than did their children. In addition, there was a positive correspondence between catharsis and having IIs for both parents and students. Hence, their IIs were cathartic and relieved anxiety for them. More than 90% of the parents had positive or mixed affect in their IIs, whereas only 59% of the students did. The students did not identify more negative emotion, but instead had more neutral IIs.

Several factors may account for this effect. Parents may feel happy for their children, recognizing to a greater extent than their children do that college will be an exciting and provocative experience. Parents may feel relief that their children chose college over other alternatives (e.g., early marriage, lower paying employment opportunities, continuing to live at home). Parents may also feel positive emotion because they are living vicariously, imagining the social and academic encounters of college life.

Another possibility is that the parents completing the SII were a unique group. Unlike many parents, these parents accompanied their children to pre-enrollment counseling, toured campus, and met administrators. Some even stayed in dorms and ate in the cafeteria. Perhaps they felt greater commitment to sending their children to college than other parents. As a result of attending the sessions, they became more familiar with campus life and could better predict what their children's lives would be like. Consequently, their anxiety may have been relieved, allowing them to focus more on the positive features of their children going to college.

THE ROLE OF IIS IN MAINTAINING LIKING AMONG ROOMMATES

We are driven by a need to belong and have others like us. Schutz's (1958) classic theory of interpersonal needs describes our necessity to satisfy inclusion, affection, and control needs. The inclusion need is concerned with establishing and maintaining rewarding interpersonal relationships that are comfortable to the persons involved with respect to the type of association and level of interaction that characterize their relationship. Affection is communicated through establishing and maintaining a rewarding interpersonal relationship characterized along dimensions of support, cooperation, sympathy, warmth, sensitivity, and generosity. Finally, the control need is the need to establish and maintain rewarding relationships that enable the persons involved to feel comfortable with the degree of power they exert over each other.

Honeycutt and Patterson (1997) investigated the relationship between II characteristics of roommate affinity among college students. Affinity seeking is a major interactional goal in initiating relationships. Yet once relationships are established, how does one sustain or maintain the friendly relationships among individuals? Affinity maintenance has been studied among wives, yet it has not received much attention among roommates even though this relationship is important due to its voluntary nature and tenuous life span.

Honeycutt and Patterson (1997) researched how IIs were used to maintain liking among college roommates. They discussed how IIs allow the preplanning of strategies for interpersonal influence and provide the mechanism by which affinity strategies are envisioned as individuals may rehearse what they will say to a roommate. IIs allow individuals to envision affinity strategies and imagine outcomes. Contingency plans may be devised if outcomes are perceived as undesirable. Honeycutt and his associates (1989) discussed how individuals imagining conversations are able to shift from an experiencing mode of cognition in which they experience the II to a reflective mode where they move out of the II to deliberate over the situation as they imagined it unfolding. Subsequently, individuals can move back into the experiencing mode. Honeycutt et al. (1992-1993) noted that, "This reflective operation may help us think more deeply about alternative outcomes to previous IIs if other messages were used" (p. 142).

Thoughts may be modified and acted on by additional thoughts similar to the way that experience is modified by new information from the environment. Affinity strategies could be substituted for messages such that IIs allow individuals to test outcomes of alternative strategies for generating or maintaining affinity. IIs allow individuals to develop as well as modify cognitive plans to accomplish goals such as seeking or maintaining affinity (cf. Berger, 1993).

Honeycutt and Patterson (1997) surveyed 84 pairs of roommates. They were given a list of strategies devised by Bell and Daly (1984) that individuals use to maintain liking in relationships. They reported how often they used each strategy as well as how often they had IIs with their roommates and the characteristics of their IIs with their roommates.

Four underlying factors of affinity maintenance were discovered. The first factor reflected other involvement. It contained the following nine strategies:

1. acting warm, caring, and empathic toward the roommate;
2. including the roommate in social activities;
3. disclosing personal information to the roommate;
4. influencing perceptions of closeness with the roommate by using nicknames;
5. spending time together with the roommate;
6. building the roommate's self-esteem through compliments
7. using nonverbal immediacy cues such as smiling at the roommate;
8. demonstrating listening and attentiveness to what the roommate is saying; and
9. rewarding association through giving the roommate gifts.

The second factor reflected rewarding communication. This factor included facilitating enjoyment such as telling stories or jokes, being a vocally animated communicator as well as being active or enthusiastic with the roommate, and presenting an interesting self by doing spontaneous things with the roommate. The third factor reflected control and included allowing the roommate to assume control in the relationship or plan activities, the self taking control or planning activities for the pair, and coming across as an independent, free thinker who is willing to express disagreement with the roommate. Finally, the last factor reflected cleanliness or orderliness, which was characterized by assisting the roommate with chores when he or she is ill and being concerned with cleanliness, order, and hygiene.

Honeycutt and Patterson (1997) found that liking for a roommate was associated with being a female, having numerous IIs with a roommate, and being able to report specific images of the scene as well as recall lines of imagined dialogue by the self or roommate. In addition, females had more pleasant IIs with their roommates than male roommates. Additional findings reveal that affinity strategies reflecting other involvement and being concerned with cleanliness were associated with the frequency of having IIs and having nondiscrepant IIs with the roommate.

The finding that females think about conversations with their roommates as well as having more positive outcomes in their internal dialogues than men is consistent with other research demonstrating that women are more likely to monitor their personal relationships. Women also are more likely to remember particular events in relationships compared with males and their knowledge of relational events or problems is higher (Harvey, Flannery, & Morgan, 1986; Honeycutt, 1995b).

Box 4.5 contains sample II journal accounts of individuals reporting on how they used IIs with their roommates to maintain the relationship.

BOX 4.5

**Sample Journal Accounts of IIs Used to Maintain
Roommate Relationships**

Subject: 24-Year-Old Female

I use IIs to maintain my relationship with my roommate. Earlier this year, my roommate Brooke and I couldn't get along. She was extremely depressed at the fact that her boyfriend was attending school in Ohio, and as a result she was horrible to be around. She was always in a bad mood, and she never wanted to leave our apartment. Furthermore, she was extremely rude to my boyfriend, an obviously jealous reaction to the happiness of our relationship. As time went by, I began to avoid Brooke, and this caused a huge stir in our relationship.

I used to imagine yelling at her about how she was ruining our friendship and that if she didn't change I was moving out. I never had the nerve to say anything to her face because I knew she was unstable and upset. Fortunately, I was wrong. My IIs were very discrepant from what actually occurred when I confronted her. She hated the fact that we were drifting apart and agreed that she needed to become more active. Since, the happiness of our relationship has dramatically increased and we go out and have fun on a regular basis. I now imagine talking to her about all the fun and tragic events that happen to me each day.

Subject: 22-Year-Old Female

Daydreaming is one of my favorite pastimes. Right now, I've been having quite a few IIs with two of my roommates. I've been told that they want to move out. However, they have not yet come to talk to me about it. They have difficulties with any sort of confrontation and find it much easier to pretend that their problems go away. During the IIs, I am usually the one confronting them, allowing myself to feel catharsis. Because this is a proactive II, I am able to put together a little script of the things I wish to say to them. However, I'm sure there will be plenty of discrepancy since I can only rehearse what I actually intend to say. These IIs also help me understand myself. I have always been the nurturing type who helps anyone close to me—I give advice, listen, and help. I don't feel unpleasant in my IIs with my roommates, just understanding as I attempt to ask them about their reasons for moving out.

SUMMARY

A major function of IIs is maintaining relationships. Individuals imagine talking with their relational partners outside of their physical presence. This compensates for the lack of physical availability at the moment in time. We frequently have IIs with our spouses and roommates.

Relational happiness is associated with positive valence as well as being engaged. This is because engaged couples are more likely to live apart and compensate for the lack of opportunity to correspond due to the physical absence. Traditionals reported more discrepant IIs than Independents. In addition, Separates were less likely to imagine positive conversations and imagined speaking more in their IIs compared with the other marital types.

Couples use IIs to rehearse telling jokes as well as enhance their attachment bonds. Furthermore, husbands tell more jokes than wives. The use of humor in marriage represents a communicative bond in which couples share inside jokes that may unite them. Attachment bonds are associated with various characteristics of IIs. A secure attachment is associated with rehearsal, low discrepancy, and high specificity, in which the relational partners can vividly recall the scene of the II as well as lines of dialogue uttered by the self and the partner. In contrast, an anxious/ambivalent attachment style is associated with discrepant IIs. Anxious attachments imagined conversations and then find that the actual interaction is different from what was imagined in the mind.

IIs are used to maintain long-distance relationships. Long-distance couples have more IIs to rehearse phone calls and to increase self- and partner-understanding. Long-distance couples report that IIs helped them maintain their relationship in the face of physical separation.

IIs are also used as a coping strategy for parents of college-bound students. Parents of college-bound students have more IIs than their college-bound children and reported more emotions in their IIs with their children. The focus of the parents seems to be the process, whereas the focus of their children was the being. Parents were sensitive to the journey of assuming individual responsibility, whereas their children were concerned with the destination or endpoint (i.e., independent living, being a college student).

Finally, research has examined IIs among roommates and their relationship to maintaining affinity or attraction in this situation. Affinity for a roommate is associated with being female, having numerous IIs with a roommate, and having specific IIs. In addition, being concerned with cleanliness as well as using affinity strategies that reflect other involvement (i.e., acting warm, caring, and empathic toward the roommate; including the roommate in social activities, using complimentary nicknames for the roommate; and disclosing personal information to the roommate) were associated with having IIs that were low in discrepancy from real conversations with the roommate.

Chapter 5

MANAGING CONFLICT:

WHY IT'S HARD TO FORGIVE AND FORGET

---

student wrote the following in her journal about recent IIs:

> In remembering past situations, I also tend to think about negative situations
> that involved conflict. Because of the emotions behind the past situations, I
> tend to remember fights and recall much detail. When I keep conflict alive in
> my mind, it allows me to relieve held-in anger. For example, I yell at my ex-
> boyfriend for all the dumb things that he did and put him in his place.

The student's II reflects what has previously been referred to as a *linked
imagined interaction* (Honeycutt, 1991). Outside of real encounters, individuals
replay prior conversations while preparing for anticipated interactions. This
chapter discusses how conflict is kept alive intrapersonally in our minds and
how it may be resolved. Individuals may use IIs to constructively deal with
conflict such as rehearsing rational arguments before anticipated encounters. II
conflict linkage theory is discussed in the following section including studies
supporting the theory.

II CONFLICT LINKAGE THEORY

In the case of long-standing conflict between parents and children, the conflict may be kept alive and maintained in the absence of the other by having retro- and proactive IIs. Although a retroactive II is experienced, it may be immediately linked with a proactive II (e.g., "Last time, I bit my lip. Next time, I see him or her, I am going to say exactly how I feel"). Given that IIs tend to occur with significant others, it may be that many of them are linked and occur between encounters reviewing and previewing conversations.

The linkage function of IIs explains recurring conflict in personal relationships. Indeed, many marital therapists lament how counseling and intervention may not result in long-term benefits in getting married couples to communicate constructively. Often there is a regression to dysfunctional patterns of communication after intervention has ended (Floyd, 1988). Conflict may be kept alive through retro- and proactive IIs that link a series of interactions. Negative emotions may be experienced as one replays the encounter (Zagacki et al., 1992).

Through the rehearsal and self-understanding functions, IIs are also used to help resolve conflict. Individuals can mull over in their minds how they will act positively, cooperatively communicate, and compromise as they attempt to reduce conflict. Yet think of a continuum ranging from desiring to reduce conflict to desiring to escalate conflict.

The linkage function of IIs for conflict helps explain why classroom instruction and counseling sessions on rational models for conflict resolution often fail as individuals regress to previous old ways for resolving conflict (e.g., "I win, you lose mentality," "I'm right, you are wrong," "I'm OK, you're not OK," "It is my way or hit the highway"). Old interaction scripts are mindlessly called up from long-term human memory. Thus, conflict episodes may pick up where they last left off despite a period of physical separation. In the meantime, the conflict has been kept alive in the mind through retro- and proactive functions of IIs.

Maintaining conflict is often done through the desire to seek revenge. Only a small proportion of people in the United States (8%) indicate that they seek revenge when they are intentionally injured (Gorsuch & Hao, 1993). Yet McCullough et al. (1998) suggested that this figure is deceptively low. Other data revealed that nearly half of all interpersonal delinquency, such as fighting at school or hurting someone badly enough to require medical attention, is motivated by revenge and anger (Pfefferbaum & Wood, 1994). McCullough et al. (1998) eloquently stated the following about revenge: "Although the base rate of seeking revenge might be rather low among all people, it seems that a substantial amount of human misery could potentially be attributed to the motive to seek revenge" (p. 1600).

Cloven and Roloff (1991) found that thinking about a problem increased beliefs about how serious the problem was. This effect was stronger when people reported that their arguments had been volatile about the issue. People reported replaying the volatile statements as well as thinking about how to attack the transgressor in future encounters. In effect, as Roloff and Ifert (1998) noted, "dwelling on the partner's negative statements does not provide a strong basis for acting in a conciliatory fashion in the future and might justify a counterattack" (p. 128).

II conflict linkage theory explains why conflict is enduring and maintained, may be constructive or destructive, and can erupt anytime in interpersonal relationships. Blalock (1969) discussed the creation of deductive theories. Axioms are propositions that are assumed to be true. Theorems are derived from reasoning and deduced from the axioms. Blalock (1969) defined *axioms* as "statements that imply direct causal links among variables" (p. 18). Theorems are testable propositions emanating from the axioms that specify associations among variables or that cause and effect are specified in terms of temporal sequence such that "x" causes "y" if it precedes it.

Honeycutt and Cantrill (2001) mentioned three axioms and nine theorems that explain mental imagery and conflict. Box 5.1 presents the theorems and axioms. Following this is a discussion of each theorem and axiom.

BOX 5.1
Axioms and Theorems of II Conflict Linkage Theory

Axiom 1: Interpersonal relationships exist through communication; the communication is the relationship; interpersonal relationships exist through thinking about the relational partner outside of actual interaction.

Axiom 2: An interpersonal relationship is thought into existence through thinking and dwelling on a potential relational partner.

Axiom 3: A major theme of interpersonal relationships is conflict management (e.g., cooperation–competition). Managing conflict begins at the intrapersonal level of communication in terms of IIs.

Theorem 1: Recurring conflict is kept alive through retro- and proactive IIs.

Theorem 2: The current mood and emotional state of individuals is associated with whether or not their IIs are positive or negative. The better a person's mood, the more positive his or her IIs will be as well as the inverse.

Corollary: These imagined interactions serve to amplify these moods, such that bad moods lead to negative IIs, which makes current moods worse, resulting in more negative IIs. Hence, the person is caught in a closed, absorbing state of emotional transference and self-fulfilling prophecies.

Theorem 3: When an individual attempts to purposely create positive IIs (i.e., as therapy for a poor marriage), negative intrusive IIs will frequently occur, in many cases with effects that undermine the therapy or positive intent.

Corollary: This intrusion results in dissonance between negative and perhaps naturally occurring IIs—intrusive IIs and positive IIs that may be artificially induced through pedagogy.

Theorem 4: Suppressed rage is a result of the lack of opportunity or inability to articulate arguments with the target of conflict.

Theorem 5: Thinking about conflict may be facilitated through exposure to contextual cues including music, chemical dependency, and media (TV shows & movies).

Theorem 6: Recurring conflict is a function of brain neurotransmitter activity in which neurons are stimulated.

Corollary: There is a biological and genetic component of conflict engagement that is reflected in neural activity.

Theorem 7: To enhance constructive conflict, individuals need to imagine positive interactions and outcomes. Thus, intrapersonal communication can be used to mollify biological determinism.

Corollary: A major function of IIs is rehearsing for anticipated encounters and relieving stress.

Theorem 8: Conflict linkage has the potential to distort reality because conflict is kept alive in a person's mind and facilitates anticipating a conversation that most likely will be discrepant from reality because the actual interaction will not occur as planned.

Theorem 9: People use IIs as a mechanism for escape from societal norms. For example, people may be expected to talk a certain way with their bosses in real life, but in their IIs, they can be considerably more bold or liberated.

Axiom 1: Interpersonal relationships exist through communication; the communication is the relationship; interpersonal relationships exist through thinking about the relational partner outside of actual interaction.

The earlier research surrounding imagined interactions sought to uncover their role in impacting interpersonal communication. Honeycutt and Cantrill (2001) suggested that often the most important determinants of relational development occur outside of immediate conversation in the cognitive realm, which includes imagined interactions. Recall from chapter 2 that IIs are with the following people in descending order: romantic partners, friends, family members, individuals in authority, people from work, ex-relational partners, and prospective partners.

Axiom 2: An interpersonal relationship is thought into existence through thinking and dwelling on a potential relationship partner.

Duck (1980) suggested that explorations of relational communication should involve interpersonal research, which looks at interpersonal relationships as they evolve outside of direct relational encounters in terms of processes such as replaying relational events during time spent alone, planning future encounters, and remembering the pleasures of encounters. The study of imagined interactions has provided for a means of investigating such phenomena (Honeycutt, 1989, 1995; Honeycutt & Cantrill, 2001). As noted in the preceding chapter, IIs can psychologically maintain relationships by concentrating thought on relational scenes and partners.

An example of keeping the relationship alive through IIs and intrapersonal communication is provided by a student from an II journal. She reported that most of her IIs were with her boyfriend and that most of these IIs were about events that happened during the day. However, her most recent II involved arguing about his choice of friends. She did not like some of his friends and previously told him that they were losers. She relived this because it was a major fight and they yelled. She remembered attacking him too harshly and often thinks about how she could have handled the situation differently. Still she reported that, although she relived this argument, most of her IIs with her boyfriend involve pleasant activities like trips she planned with him.

Axiom 3: A major theme of interpersonal relationships is conflict management (e.g., cooperation–competition). Managing conflict begins at the intrapersonal level of communication in terms of IIs.

Honeycutt (1995) noted the possibility of identifying relational themes by analyzing the linked imagined interactions that involve the replay of prior encounters while preparing for anticipated interactions. However, research directed toward this specific purpose is sparse.

Honeycutt and Wiemann (1999) alluded to this axiom in their research that includes Fitzpatrick's marital typology. Research suggests that certain marital types share certain themes. Traditional couples have more communal and sharing themes compared with Independent, Separate, or Mixed couple types. Of course, research specifically demonstrating the use of themes reflecting conflict and the use of IIs in creating and maintaining the themes is lacking. Certainly research, including the marital typologies, could be an approach to uncovering such specific ideas because one of the key dimensions of the typology is that of conflict (Fitzpatrick, 1988).

Allen and Berkos (1998) found support for Axiom 3 and Theorem 1. They examined the themes of imagined conflict and how conflict was maintained through retroactive IIs. They defined communication episodes as routines that have identifiable openings and closing (Pearce & Cronen, 1980). Watzlawick, Beavin, and Jackson (1967) asserted that communication episodes are punctuated perceptually by individuals in the episodes. Retroactive IIs serve a cognitive reviewing function in which individuals punctuate communication episodes. Communication episodes in interpersonal relationships occur between interaction partners and within individuals as they attempt to understand a string of behavior and/or define the relationship.

In examining the punctuation and themes of conflict, Allen and Berkos (1998) surveyed 105 students at California State University, Long Beach ranging in age from 21 to 55 who averaged 26 years. They surveyed 54% women and 46% men. Participants were given a weekly journal assignment asking them to identify certain dimensions and functions of their IIs. Two research assistants analyzed the journals and decided whether the communication episodes were conflictual or nonconflictual, whom they were with, and if the level of conflict was behavioral, normative, or personal.

Behavioral conflict involves disagreement about specific behaviors such as different preferences for music, art, or recreation (Braiker & Kelley, 1979). Normative conflict involves disagreement over relational rules and norms such as household duties and balancing finances. Personal conflicts concern an individual's personality, attitudes, values, and preferences.

The data reveal that out of 774 imagined interaction episodes, 41% were conflictual. Most of the conflicts were with intimate relational partners (27%) followed by friends and bosses (both 18%). A few were with co-workers (8%) and roommates (7%). Furthermore, one third of the conflictual IIs was linked to some previous conflict that the participant had recorded in the journal. Normative (38%) and personal (37%) conflict were more frequent than behavioral conflict (24%). Kroll-Mensing (1992) also found that the IIs of anxious and depressed individuals were more conflict focused compared with nonanxious, nondepressed individuals. She also found that getting even was associated with anxiety. Furthermore, anxiety and depression were associated with having IIs that explored causes of conflict in hopes of developing persuasive arguments.

Theorem 1: Recurring conflict is kept alive through retro- and proactive IIs.

A study conducted by Johnson and Roloff (1998) was conducted as a means to assess factors contributing to the problem of serial arguing in relationships and its effects on relationship quality. Serial arguing occurs when individuals repeatedly argue over issues. In looking at the factors affecting perceptions of resolvability of a given conflict, they found that perceived resolvability was negatively associated with the following items:

1. arguments arising from violated expectations,
2. countercomplaining and partner-initiated demand–withdrawal,

3. predictability of argumentative episodes,
4. overall discord,
5. withdrawal after a conflict episode, and
6. mulling over the argument.

The relevant factor from this study in relation to conflict linkage is the last item—mulling. *Mulling* refers to mentally reliving the argument repeatedly and involves the use of retroactive IIs.

Recall from the preceding chapter that the oral history interview is a semistructured narrative that allows married couples to reconstruct events from the relationship's past. Spouses' imagined conversations include issues of conflict. There is regret at not having said things that are on one's mind. This replaying involves the use of retroactive IIs, with proactive IIs being used to rehearse for the next encounter with the spouse, such that the conflict picks up where it was left.

Klos and Singer (1981) conducted a classic study on conflict linkage and IIs by inducing IIs in adolescents as a means to elicit emotions about parental conflict. Their purpose was to study the determinants of adolescents' ongoing thought following simulated parental confrontations. They looked at the effects of resolved versus unresolved situations with parents, mutual nonconflictual parental interaction versus mutual conflictual interaction, and simulated coercive parental interaction versus simulated collaborative parental interaction.

Proposing that exposure through simulated interaction to these conditions would later affect recurrence of simulation-relevant thoughts, the researchers had individuals participate in one of six conditions:

1. Collaborative decision making with parent, resolved.
2. Collaborative decision making with parent, unresolved.
3. Collaborative confrontation with parent, resolved.
4. Collaborative confrontation with parent, unresolved.
5. Coercive confrontation with parent, resolved.
6. Coercive confrontation with parent, unresolved.

The participants engaged in simulated interactions with a parent while they were read a predeveloped parental script for the appropriate situation. The participants were asked to think about the last visit with the same-sex parent that was 3 days or longer in duration.

Each of the conditions were described as follows: *coercive confrontation* involved a parent trying to win an argument without listening to the subject's viewpoint, whereas *collaborative confrontation* involved a parent expressing her or his viewpoint while trying to understand the subject's viewpoint. *Collaborative decision making* involved a parent and subject working together to find a solution to a shared interpersonal problem external to the relationship. *Resolution/nonresolution* focused on whether subjects were able to reach a solution at the end of three imagined interactions.

After the IIs, subjects were taken to a separate room and given a 20-minute period in which thought samples were elicited by sounding a buzzer at 20 random intervals. At each interval, subjects were to report their thoughts, feelings, and mental images. Thoughts were coded as *simulation related* if they were directly relevant to the simulation conditions. Affect was measured before and after the simulations using 5-point Likert that reflected interest, anger, distress, joy, disgust, and contempt. Stress with parents was also measured by items, which assessed the level of interpersonal conflict and need satisfaction including acceptance, recognition, and support.

Anger was higher in the coercive, as opposed to collaborative, conditions. Once exposed to a simulated parental conflict, students with a history of stress with parents reported as much as 50% of their later thoughts concerning the simulations. Klos and Singer (1981) concluded that a reawakening of unpleasant past experiences is enough to sustain arousal and recurrent thought even if the conflict is resolved. Their research appears to lend credence to the idea that conflict is kept alive through proactive and retroactive IIs. It could be that the thoughts of adolescents who have a history of parental stress could be so unpleasant as a result of environmental cues, such as TV plots and films, that it provokes recurrent thoughts of conflict. Whether an episode is resolved or unresolved depends on the particular records that are evoked by the situation and their reconstitution in the given scenario. That is, resolution is contingent on the retroactive IIs that are recalled and the ways in which they are transformed through the use of proactive IIs. Long-standing child–parent conflict may be kept alive and maintained as a result.

Roloff and Ifert (1998) discussed how individuals are able to control the conversational behaviors that can occur in future encounters. Individuals are able to identify factors that set off a conflict and avoid future confrontations. For example, abused wives use conflict avoidance as a frequent long-term coping device (Gelles & Straus, 1988). This often involves avoiding the partner at certain times, avoiding the volatile issues, or shifting the conversation away from the issues.

Yet individuals may think about introducing prior conversations into the current encounter. Having thought about a prior conflict, an individual may engage the partner with the intent of retaliating (Roloff & Ifert, 1998). Alternatively, having thought about a barrier to gaining compliance, the individual may have thought about new ways to overcome it and deliberately raise it in a later encounter. In these cases, a new encounter picks up where an earlier one left off (Roloff & Ifert, 1998).

Theorem 1 is represented in a journal account by a student who reported on a recent II with her roommate regarding bills. The roommate complained about a laundry bill. When the roommate confronted her, the student ignored the roommate, which made the roommate angry and she used profanity. The student had retroactive IIs about this scene in terms of what she should have said to the roommate after being called names. The student also reported how she simultaneously had a proactive II in terms of planning what to say to the roommate if any future confrontations occurred.

> **Theorem 2: The current moods and emotional states of individuals are associated with whether their IIs are positive or negative. The better a person's mood, the more positive his or her IIs will be as well as the inverse.**

> **Corollary: These IIs serve to amplify these moods, such that bad moods lead to negative IIs, which makes current moods worse, resulting in more negative IIs. Hence, the person is caught in a closed, absorbing state of emotional transference and self-fulfilling prophecies.**

Gilligan and Bower (1984) asserted that prevailing moods influence thoughts and those particular thoughts elicit relevant mood states. Perhaps the prevailing mood determines whether an individual chooses to reflect on positive or negative IIs depending on their current emotional state. This finding suggests that IIs help with the identification and clarification of emotional responses to situations. Yet the reversal may be true—emotional states affect imagined interactions. Hence, IIs and emotions affect each other.

An example is a student reporting in an II journal how she harbors anger after her boyfriend broke up with her a few months ago without giving an explanation. The student reported how she *hates* him and has imagined several times what she will do if she sees him again. She plans to curse him and even imagines throwing a drink on him.

Recall from chapter 3 that the results of the research conducted by Zagacki and his associates (1992) reveal that emotions are a vital feature of IIs. The emotion associated with IIs is integrally related to the partner with whom the conversation is held and to the topic of the II. Once an interaction has taken place, an individual may feel better after reviewing the encounter or he or she may use IIs prior to an encounter, perhaps through means of rehearsal, to lessen tension and uncertainty.

In their study, Zagacki et al. (1992) found that mixed emotions (both positive and negative) are associated with greater II activity and retroactivity than positive emotions. Negative emotions are associated with lower levels of pleasantness, more discrepancy, and greater self-dominance. Again this seems to suggest that IIs low in pleasantness, most likely involving conflict, are associated with negative emotions.

Whether an individual's emotional state is causally linked to her or his II experiences or whether a person's imagined interactions affect her or his emotional state is a question that necessitates further investigation. However, research suggests that the nature of IIs is a function of the communicator's situational experiences (Zagacki et al., 1992). If a person is currently not experiencing stressful activities or relationships, IIs are likely to involve mixed imagery, which have been shown to be more pleasant. However, if a person is experiencing conflict, then his or her IIs are likely to be of a primarily verbal mode and less pleasant.

The study by Zagacki et al. (1992) yielded results suggesting that IIs associated with positive emotions occur less frequently and with lower levels of retroactivity than IIs having mixed emotions. The researchers note the surprising nature of such findings in that one might expect persons to dwell on pleasant communicative episodes to extend the benefit of positive feelings. However, the findings actually suggest that individuals do not engage in such II activity. Rather, once pleasant communicative experiences are acknowledged, they are simply taken for granted and not often recalled. Another possibility is that individuals avoid reviewing what they perceive to have been pleasant communicative episodes for fear of finding potentially discrepant information, which could possibly lead to an unpleasant state.

Additional support for Theorem 2 can be found in psychological studies on rumination. Self-focused rumination occurs when people repetitively focus on themselves and the cause and implications of negative feelings (Lyubomirsky, Tucker, Caldwell, & Berg, 1999). Rumination is associated with depression, hopelessness, and lack of motivations. Rumination enhances negative thinking and poor problem solving (Nolen-Hoeksema, 1991). Lyubomirsky and her associates (1999) reported how depressed individuals are insecure and pessimistic while ruminating. They may even acknowledge that there are ways to solve their problems, but feel they do not have the energy to do so. Essentially, these individuals are in a closed self-fulfilling prophecy loop in which they are focusing on their problems and blaming themselves, but feel further depressed at their lack of resources and motivation to alleviate their problems. They view their problems as more overwhelming and stressful than they really are. Additional studies on rumination also reveal that people who seek revenge against offenders report more rumination and are more likely to retaliate following threats to their self-esteem (Collins & Bell, 1997; Stuckless & Goranson, 1992).

Theorem 3: When an individual attempts to purposely create positive IIs (i.e., as therapy for a poor marriage), negative intrusive IIs will frequently occur, in many cases with effects that undermine the therapy or positive intent.

Corollary: This intrusion results in dissonance between negative and perhaps naturally occurring IIs—intrusive IIs and positive IIs that may be artificially induced through pedagogy.

Honeycutt (1995) noted that many marital therapists lament how counseling and intervention may not result in long-term benefits in getting married couples to communicate constructively. Furthermore, Floyd (1988) suggested that there is often regression to dysfunctional patterns of communication after intervention has ended. In addition, Hatfield (1982) noted the difficulty that the counselor as well as the distressed couple may have when attempting to talk about marital problems. Articulating the feelings of being unloved and remediating problems associated with such feelings is a difficult task. Yet the difficulty may be dealt with by having discrepant IIs or having compensatory IIs that are used to communicate some of the problems not openly discussed.

An explanation for the intrusion of negative IIs is the fact that II pleasantness has been found to be negatively associated with memory (Honeycutt et al., 1992-1993). Thus, IIs accompanied by more negative affect are more memorable than more pleasant IIs. Perhaps this explains why negative information, or IIs, may be recalled more readily and have higher informational value than positive information, or IIs. Attempting to purposefully create positive IIs while ruminating about conflict may be difficult.

Theorem 4: Suppressed rage is a result of the lack of opportunity or inability to articulate arguments with the target of conflict.

Investigation of aggression types has led to a more specific exploration of a certain type of aggression known as verbal aggression (Infante, Chandler, & Rudd, 1989; Infante & Rancer, 1996). The research has centered on the concept of verbal aggression as opposed to argumentativeness in approaching conflict. Along that line, the primary difference between argumentation and verbal aggression has been identified as the locus of attack (Infante & Wigley, 1986). *Argumentativeness* is defined as the presentation and defense of one's positions on controversial issues while attacking the positions taken by others on issues. The locus of attack here is the message. *Verbal aggression*, while possibly incorporating attacks on the message, differs in that it also includes personal attacks or attacks on the other's self-concept. As one can see, the locus of attack for the verbally aggressive person is the messenger. Argumentativeness, then, is seen as a more constructive way to address conflict, and verbal aggression is a more destructive, less constructive way to address conflict (Infante et al., 1989).

More than a decade's worth of research in this area has been conducted to explicate the differences of argumentativeness and verbal aggression in the handling of conflict (Infante & Rancer, 1996). This was done as a means to understand the communicative catalysts to physical violence (Infante & Wigley, 1986). Infante and Wigley suggested that verbal aggression and argumentativeness are two distinctively different constructs. They are unrelated and only yield a correlation of -.04. This communication-oriented approach asserts that destructive forms of communication, including verbal aggression, lead to physical violence, whereas constructive forms, including argumentativeness, reduce the likelihood that social conflict will escalate to physical violence (Infante et al., 1989). These findings suggest that, although not all verbal aggression leads to physical violence, the correlation between verbal aggression and physical violence ($r = .32$, $p < .001$) indicates that there is a moderate, but nonetheless, shared relationship (Infante & Wigley, 1986).

Infante et al. (1989) formalized a theory that explains verbal aggression in terms of one's lack of communication skills in devising an argument that deals with the point of conflict, rather than verbally attacking the person with whom one is in conflict. This has been labeled the *argumentative skills deficiency model*. Research has approached the study of aggression in interpersonal communication from this perspective (Infante & Wigley, 1986).

Research by Infante et al. (1989) serves to support the idea that inability to articulate arguments with a target of conflict causes increased levels of arousal. As rage mounts, verbal aggression intensifies, possibly culminating in physical violence. If a person experiences heightened arousal but stops short of physical violence, the result can be suppressed rage.

Addressing the idea of increased arousal leading to violence, Zillmann (1983) discussed the notion of *excitation transfer*. According to this idea, a verbally aggressive act produces negative emotional reaction such as anger and a covert verbal response, which facilitates recall of the emotional experience at a later date. From this description, it seems likely that imagined interactions may aid in the recollection process. Zillmann suggested that the trace of negative affect left behind (perhaps revisited through the use of IIs) can combine additively with subsequent verbally aggressive acts. "Basically, residues of excitation from previous verbally aggressive acts, if not dissipated, intensify intentions to behave aggressively toward the origin of the verbal aggression" (Infante et al., 1989, p. 165). As noted previously, a factor that serves to perpetuate residual excitation is the retroactive imagined interaction.

Recently, I have begun testing Infante and Wigley's (1986) contention that the inability or lack of opportunity to articulate arguments with a target of conflict causes increased levels of arousal. As rage mounts, verbal aggression intensifies, possibly culminating in physical violence. A path model was tested that contained the following characteristics of IIs: valence, frequency, proactivity, specificity, discrepancy, and self-dominance. Three functions of IIs were tested in the model: catharsis, self-understanding, and conflict-linkage. I sampled students in long-term relationships who were either dating or married. The participants consisted of 126 individuals (58 males and 68 females). The mean age of the sample was 23.95 and ranged from 18 to 52 years. Persons knew their partners an average of 6 years (range: 4 months to 36 years, $SD = 93.17$) and averaged 4 years, 7 months exclusively seeing them.

FIG. 5.1. Path model of II characteristics, verbal aggression, and coercion.

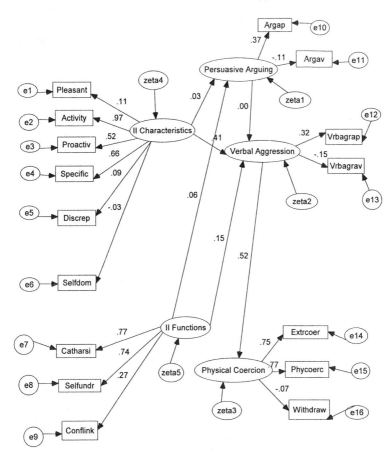

Figure 5.1 presents the path diagram of the model. The circles represent unmeasured variables not actually measured. The feature of this analysis allows us to determine which variables best represent the theoretical construct. For example, the II characteristic *oval* represents some of the features of IIs that were discussed in chapter 2. The data reveal that, in the context of measuring verbal and physical aggression, activity, proactivity, and specificity best reflect the characteristics of IIs that are important in predicting verbal aggression. The higher the number, the more the variable predicts the theoretical construct in a positive or negative direction. Similarly, as revealed in Figure 5.1, catharsis and self-understanding are the most important functions of IIs in predicting verbal aggression.

Persuasive arguing was reflected by items indicating a tendency to either approach arguments (e.g., "Arguing over controversial issues improves my intelligence," "I am energetic and enthusiastic when I argue," "I have the ability to do well in an argument") or items indicating a tendency to avoid arguments (e.g., "I enjoy avoiding arguments"; Infante & Rancer, 1982). Arguing with a person creates more problems than it solves. ("I find myself unable to think of effective points during an argument"). As expected, the best indicator of persuasive arguing was approaching arguments.

Verbal aggression was measured using Infante and Wigley's (1986) verbal aggression measure consisting of 10 items (e.g., "When individuals are very stubborn, I use insults to soften the stubbornness," "When individuals insult me, I get a lot of pleasure out of really telling them off," "When nothing seems to work in trying to influence others, I yell and scream in order to get some movement from them"). Another 10 items reflected avoiding verbal aggression (e.g., "I am extremely careful to avoid attacking individuals' intelligence when I attack their ideas," "When people criticize my shortcomings I take it in good humor and do not try to get back at them," "When an argument shifts to personal attacks I try very hard to change the subject").

Physical coercion was measured using the Straus (1990) Conflict Tactics Scale (CTS). This scale measures reasoning, verbal aggression, and physical coercion as methods of dealing with relational conflict. For reasoning tactics, respondents are asked how often during the past year they discussed issues calmly, got information to back up their position, or tried to bring in someone to help settle things. Verbal aggression is measured by reports of insults or swearing, sulking or refusing to talk about an issue, leaving the room, spiting the partner, and threatening to hit or throw something. The use of insults, swearing, and spiting the partner is reflected in Infante and Wigley's (1986) verbal aggression measure. Physical coercion represents actually throwing something, pushing, grabbing, shoving, slapping, kicking, biting, hitting, choking, threatening to use a gun or knife, and actually using a gun or knife.

We measured the underlying dimensions of the CTS and found that there were three dimensions or factors. Extreme coercion represents choking the partner and using a gun or knife. Physical coercion represents slapping the partner, throwing something at him or her, kicking, biting, hitting, pushing, grabbing, or shoving the partner. Withdrawal represents stomping out of the room, refusing to talk about an issue, saying something to spite the partner, or trying to bring someone in to help settle things. Physical coercion is best reflected by extreme coercion and the less intense forms of physical coercion such as slapping or pushing.

II characteristics of activity (frequency), proactivity, and specificity impact on verbal aggression as revealed by the regression coefficient of .41. However, II characteristics did not impact on persuasive arguments. A possible explanation for this is the slight path from II functions to verbal aggression (.15). The path diagram reflects how catharsis and self-understanding reflect II functions that impact on verbal aggression. Perhaps individuals who imagine being verbally aggressive as opposed to thinking about rational arguments let off steam (catharsis) while also believing that they understand their rage better. The path diagram results also support Infante and Wigley's (1986) contention of a direct link between verbal aggression and physical coercion. In an alternative model, persuasive arguing did not predict physical coercion (-.08), and functions of IIs were negatively associated with physical coercion (-.20) as well as characteristics of IIs being negatively associated with physical coercion (-.30).

Makela (1992) also reported on the correlation between verbal aggression and the use of verbally aggressive IIs. Participants were given the SII (see chap. 2 appendix), the verbal aggression measure by Infante and Wigley (1986), and a description of a persuasion situation including a highly argumentative adversary. This description included an adversary's use of three verbal aggressive messages: ridicule, character attack, and competence attack using Infante and Wigley's descriptions.

Participants were told to imagine that they had a casual friend who was highly argumentative. They enjoyed discussing controversial issues and considered arguing an exciting intellectual challenge. You are living on campus and are unhappy with the quality of food served in the cafeterias. You decide to collect signatures on petitions and present the petitions to an appropriate university administrator. You want your friend to help you by getting 50 signatures on one of the petitions. You ask, "Would you circulate this petition for me?" While rolling his or her eyes, he or she replies: "Well, I don't think so. Why would you want to do something like that anyhow?" Imagine your response to your friend and write your hypothetical response. The eye rolls indicate ridicule according to Infante and Wigley (1986).

Participants wrote down an II. However, after doing this, the participants were told that the friend says, "I think you greatly exaggerated the problem. I don't think it is that serious and you are foolish for getting so upset about something like this." This represented a character attack. Again, they wrote an II to this response. Finally, the friend responded, "Look even if there is a problem, you would have to be insane to think your plan of circulating petitions is going to solve the problem." This represented a competence attack. A final II was written.

The results reveal that people high in verbal aggression reported more instances of themselves engaging in verbally aggressive communication in their IIs compared with people low in verbal aggression in response to ridicule. Similar results were found for the responses to character and competence attacks. Makela (1992) concluded that less skilled arguers could sustain constructive conflict by planning and rehearsing arguments through proactive IIs. She speculated that a high verbal aggressor may be able to decrease the level of negative affect in a conflict by constructing and rehearsing arguments through IIs.

Theorem 5: Thinking about conflict may be facilitated through exposure to contextual cues including music, chemical dependency, and media (TV shows and movies).

Support for this theorem can be found in the research by Murphy and O'Farrell (1994), which looked at the factors associated with marital aggression in male alcoholics. According to their research, binge drinking is associated with coercive marital conflict. Thus, when alcohol is consumed, marital aggression is a likely outcome for male alcoholics. The study also found that maritally aggressive men exhibit more verbal aggression and higher alcohol use as well as less confidence in their ability to manage interpersonal conflict without drinking. These findings seem to suggest support for the association between alcohol consumption and conflict as well as support for the provocation of thought about conflict by the use of alcohol.

Music influences conflict as individuals hear songs, recall old conflicts, and relive the arguments. Music therapy is an entire field of study in which music is used to improve emotional, physical, physiological, and spiritual well being. Being a musician and drummer myself, I personally attest to how music affects emotions. The brain's neurotransmitters are affected by the tempo of the music. Smeijsters (1995) discussed the functions of music in music therapy and described content analyses of music therapy students. For example, they write in their journals how music is sentimental in that "it works like a dream, it evokes pleasant worlds, but also nightmares and repulsion" (Smeijsters, 1995, p. 387). This reflects the valence characteristic of IIs. Smeijsters presented data indicating how 41% of individuals reporting on the functions of music in their lives report that it reminds them of their past. Some of the most common functions were: using music to get into a better mood (65%), experiencing pleasure (50%), experiencing pain (50%), venting frustrations (41%), and getting physiologically aroused (62%).

The ISO principle of music therapy indicates that music can be selected to gradually change the mood of a person (Honeycutt & Eidenmuller, 2001). If you are angry, start with music that is loud. Later switch to a more tranquil piece of music. The vectoring power of music is that we change the mood or emotion of persons from one affective pole (joy) to its opposite (anger) through small incremental changes in the rhythm and intensity of the music. Hence, music can be used to facilitate emotional learning by serving as a vehicle for the appropriate expression of emotions.

The top three functions of music are influencing moods and emotions, helping with stress management, and being used as an expressive outlet. People have retroactive and proactive IIs when listening to certain types of music (Honeycutt & Eidenmuller, 2001). The melody or lyrics of songs may take individuals to different scenes of interaction with significant others. In fact, a classic Four Tops song called, "It's the Same Old Song," expounds on how the memory of music affects current emotions (i.e., "You've gone and left my heart in pain. All you've left is our favorite song, the one we danced too all night long which brings sweet memories of all the tender love that used to be").

Theorem 6: Recurring conflict is a function of brain neurotransmitter activity in which neurons are stimulated.

Corollary: There are biological and genetic components of conflict engagement that are reflected in neural activity.

Although music affects the brain's neurotransmitters, recent proposals by McCroskey (1997) and others indicate the importance of biological factors in determining communication traits such as communication apprehension (Beatty, McCroskey, & Heisel, 1998) and verbal aggression (Beatty & McCroskey, 1997). Beatty and his colleagues (1998) believe that from 50% to 80% of communication apprehension is explained by genetic factors. The idea to be drawn from this research is support for the idea that there is a biological link to conflict. If certain communicative characteristics such as communication apprehension can be linked to biological determinants, then it seems logical that the likelihood to engage in conflict could be linked to such factors as well.

In delineating their rationale for a biologically rooted explanation for verbal aggression framed in the nature versus nurture argument, Beatty and McCroskey (1997) stated that from their reductionist approach, cognition cannot and does not exist independently of neurological operation and cognition is triggered by neurological activity. According to them, "theories that posit cognitive and emotional processes that do not correspond to neurological functioning are probably wrong, regardless of how intuitively appealing the theories might seem" (Beatty & McCroskey, 1997, p. 449). Thus, any explanation of a cognitive phenomenon such as that of conflict in terms of linked IIs must acknowledge the impact of neurology.

Beatty and McCroskey (1997) posited that much of the prior research in the area of verbal aggression has focused on the social learning paradigm. This approach has ignored the work of psychobiologists that strongly points to the biological influence on such traits as verbal aggression. The primary thesis of the work of Beatty and McCroskey (1997) is that verbal aggression is an inborn trait that exists long before social influences affect learning processes, and thus is independent of social learning.

Such an argument suggesting that verbal aggression is linked to a biological explanation rather than a social learning or conditioning explanation could, it appears, be extrapolated to the existence of a more general conflict-engaging nature. Those who engage more often in conflict may experience more IIs that link conflicts together, thus experiencing more conflict.

Theorem 7: To enhance constructive conflict, individuals need to imagine positive interactions and outcomes. Thus, intrapersonal communication can be used to mollify biological determinism.

Corollary: A major function of IIs is rehearsing for anticipated encounters and relieving stress.

The study linking characteristics and functions of IIs with persuasive arguing, verbal aggression, and physical coercion in support of Theorem 4 also had some data measuring relationship happiness. Individuals reported how happy they were in their current relationship. Relationship happiness was predicted by having pleasant IIs and avoiding the conflict linkage function of IIs. In other words, the more an individual kept thinking about conflict with a partner, the less happy he or she was in the relationship.

Infante and Rancer (1996) noted in their review of research on the topics of argumentativeness and verbal aggression that, in taking a trait approach such as with this line of research, the concern becomes how personality traits and communication predispositions can be modified. They acknowledged that traits such as communication apprehension have been affected favorably by programs that focus on cognitive orientations and skill development. Such intervention, they suggested, seems possible for verbal aggression as well. Therefore, if these traits can be positively affected by training such that biological determinism can be mollified, this seems to provide support indirectly for the notion that constructive conflict techniques can be taught.

In his work examining verbal aggression, Infante (1995) took the approach that the prevention of verbal aggression can be achieved through communication skills training. He noted that abuse prevention programs taking a communication skills approach have been tested successfully with distressed and abusive couples. The central premise of the skill's approach is that physical and verbal abuse will be less likely to occur when individuals are proficiently trained communicators.

Although studies cited in the support of Theorem 6 reveal that much of the cause for some communicative attributes is attributed to biological factors, there is still variance that can be explained by environmental factors. For that reason, IIs can be used to overcome some biological determinism. With the proactive tendency of IIs, individuals can aid themselves in initially preparing points and counterpoints of conflict in the most constructive way possible. Conversely, most individuals have discrepant IIs that enhance conflict.

A prototypical example of this is provided by a student writing about her friend, Eve, for a journal assignment on IIs. Eve's IIs tend to be unpleasant as well as being conflictual. Eve is viewed by her friends having a polite encounter filled with pleasantries and small talk with a mutual friend. After the mutual friend leaves, Eve asks questions like, "Did you see how she smiled after she asked me what I have been doing?" Eve believes the smile was a putdown and questions how something was phrased to her and wonders if it was meant to be an insult.

Eve's behavior reflects Theorem 7 because her negative IIs do not result in constructive conflict. The student friend indicated how the majority of Eve's were retroactive and unproductive. Eve distrusts others and is often unwilling to take a conversation at its face value. Instead, she searches for the hidden meaning behind the words of others that is often discrepant from their intent.

Individuals may imagine forgiving others who have offended them. Forgiveness occurs when individuals do not want to avoid the offender and see harm coming to the offending partner (McCullough et al., 1998). Forgiving is associated with a willingness to sacrifice for the relationship, empathy, judgments of blame, lack of rumination, perceived intentionality, severity, and avoidability of the offense (Boon & Sulsky, 1997; Girard & Mullet, 1997). Conversely, revenge is associated with rumination and dwelling on negative thoughts (McCullough et al., 1998).

Several studies have suggested that IIs can be used strategically to rehearse anticipated encounters and to relieve stress (e.g., in such settings as forensics competition; Gotcher & Honeycutt, 1989; Honeycutt & Gotcher, 1991). Participants involved in forensics competition must be aware of the communication environment and in control of the messages they convey because the nature of such a form of competition is that those most adept at doing so receive the highest rewards (Honeycutt & Gotcher, 1991). Gotcher and Honeycutt (1989) sought to evaluate how forensics participants use IIs in competition. They found that competitors used IIs for rehearsal for potential situations (Gotcher, & Honeycutt, 1989). This suggests that IIs can be used to practice possible messages even when several possibilities exist for playing out the interaction (Honeycutt & Gotcher, 1991).

Another of Gotcher and Honeycutt's (1989) findings suggest that higher frequency IIs decreases discrepancy, alluding to the increased ability to construct an imagined situation that closely mirrors reality through the use of IIs (Honeycutt & Gotcher, 1991). Proactive IIs were correlated with imagined success during competition rounds, but not with actual success (Gotcher & Honeycutt, 1989). The use of IIs appears to aid competitors in psychologically preparing for actual competition and may serve to create success through self-fulfilling prophecy (Honeycutt & Gotcher, 1991).

Imagined interactions have also been used by such individuals as those engaged in volatile political protest (Petress, 1990, and in preparing for cross-cultural university admission interviews, Petress, 1995). Studying the use of IIs by student protesters present at the Tian-an-men Square demonstrations in Beijing, China, Petress (1990) indicated that students present during the riots engaged in the use of IIs for such purposes as rehearsing and preparing scripts. The prepared scripts (in case they were taken in for interrogation by the authorities), the rehearsal of conversations with family members and friends enabling the student to remain calm during the riots, and reflecting on actual experiences and interactions endured after the riots were stopped. This is discussed in more detail in chapter 7 when discussing cross-cultural II studies.

Theorem 8: Conflict linkage has the potential to distort reality because conflict is kept alive in a person's mind and facilitates the anticipation of a conversation that most likely will be discrepant from reality because the actual interaction will not occur as planned.

Discrepancy is the II characteristic that provides for the incongruity between IIs and the actual interaction they addressed. Recall from chapter 2 that research suggests that individuals who are chronically lonely have been found to have highly discrepant IIs, which researchers suggest serves to perpetuate their lonely state (Edwards et al., 1988). Lonely people have limited prior interactions on which to base their IIs, so any they experience prior to new interaction are likely to be high in discrepancy.

Support for this theorem can be found in the reported finding that verbally based IIs are less pleasant (Zagacki et al., 1992). These less pleasant IIs concern conflict and are usually more verbal, as opposed to visual, in nature. Zagacki et al. (1992) noted that verbally based IIs are usually less similar to the actual communication they represent. Thus, through a syllogistic approach, if conflictual IIs are more verbal and verbally based IIs are usually discrepant, then conflictual IIs are more discrepant, thus distorting reality.

Theorem 9: People utilize IIs as a mechanism for escape from societal norms. For example, people may be expected to talk a certain way with their bosses in real life, but in their IIs, they can be considerably more bold or more liberated.

As noted in chapter 3, there is research indicating that IIs compensate for the lack of real interaction. In their discussion of IIs used for therapeutic purposes, Rosenblatt and Meyer (1986) discussed how an individual may use IIs in place of actually confronting a loved one in fear that the loved one would be hurt by the message. Recall the catharsis function from chapter 3 in which IIs allow individuals to release suppressed feelings. Yet after catharsis is released, Roloff and Ifert (1998) speculated that some individuals might lack the motivations to actually confront the transgressor. They also speculated that the rehearsal function might inhibit seeking compliance. If an individual anticipates negative responses from the partner, then he or she might not formulate or even abandon a compliance goal. Ifert and Roloff (1994) found that, prior to making a request for assistance, individuals anticipate the possible barriers for gaining compliance. Similarly, in conflict situations, a partner's anticipated aggressive response to a problem may inhibit discussion about the problem (Cloven & Roloff, 1993).

Honeycutt (1989) discussed the use of IIs as a means of compensation by the elderly who may not see their loved ones as often as they would like. The research focusing on geographically separated individuals and their increased use of IIs during separation for the purposes of coping is additional indirect support for the notion that IIs are used in place of real interaction. Future research should investigate this idea of compensation in more conflictual situations, which may inhibit real interaction, such as with disagreements between an employee and employer.

Although some of the proposed theorems and corollaries appear to have significant support as existing in current literature, other areas have only indirect or negligible support and thus need additional research to support them. Conflict linkage theory holds great potential for explaining the effects of cognition outside of actual interaction on real-life relationships, and its axiomatic approach makes for a logical and sensible explanation for the perpetuation of conflict in interpersonal relationships. Through continued research efforts, a greater understanding of the causes of conflict can be achieved.

IIS ABOUT ARGUING AMONG MARITAL TYPES

Gendrin and Werner (1996-1997) examined the role of IIs in processing marital disputes. Using Fitzpatrick's (1988) Relational Dimensions Instruments, couples were identified as Traditionals, Independents, and Separates. Recall from chapter 4 that Traditionals are high on companionship and sharing and have few constraints on undifferentiated space. Independents actively argue, yet disclose positive and negative feelings to each other. Their space is differentiated and they do not share similar time schedules.

Separates hold conventional values like the Traditionals in terms of espousing family and marriage while supporting individual freedom. They have less companionship and maintain individual spaces more than the other two types. Separates are emotionally divorced and seek reinforcement outside the marriage while experiencing little direct conflict in their marriage.

The couples were surveyed to think about conflict situations that they might imagine before or after an actual interaction. Gendrin and Werner (1996-1997) surveyed 216 couples: 39% Traditionals, 23% Independents, and 26% Separates. The remaining couples were mixed types that were not included in their data analysis because of the small percentage (12%). Mixed types consisted of a spouse endorsing a given marriage type and the partner endorsing a different one.

The data reveal that Separates had more IIs about conflict than both Independents and Traditionals. They also imagined disagreements before actual interactions with their partners, and they reviewed them after they took place. The Separates' proactive IIs were unpleasant, whereas their retroactive imagined disagreements were more neutral in terms of emotional affect. Gendrin and Werner (1996-97) surmised that Separates use a hit-and-run tactic in conflict situations, which consists of confronting the partner with hostility and withdrawing thereafter.

The lack of emotional reaction in the Separates' retroactive imagined disagreements could be viewed as a sign of relief that they avoided a full-fledged argument. Considering that Separates are unable to coordinate either conflict engagement or conflict avoidance, this type of II plays a dysfunctional role for them. Gendrin and Werner (1996-1997) stated, "Not only are Separates unable to talk things out with their partners, they relive, in their minds, the emotional roller coaster of their brief encounters with one another" (p. 135).

This type of II may reflect the need for Separates to cooperate to bring a tense discussion to an end. For example, a partner may raise his or her voice, forcing the other partner to withdraw knowing that the partner cannot continue the confrontation. Both partners may be fearful of actual confrontation and cooperate to stop the argument. Yet, IIs may reinforce this tactic, making it difficult to develop a plan for dealing with serious issues. For Separates, mulling about marital conflicts may create a self-fulfilling prophecy that partners cannot talk to each other, resulting in unhappiness with the marriage. Gendrin and Werner (1996-1997) also found that Traditionals reported more marital happiness than Separates or Independents.

Conversely, thinking about conflict was helpful for the Independents. Not only do they imagine themselves frequently in disagreements with their partners, they also rehearse what they are going to say before actual encounters and have retroactive IIs after actual conflict episodes. Gendrin and Werner (1996-1997) also discussed how Independents' lack of emotional negativity prior to arguments was due to mentally engaging in the conflict rather than avoiding it. Independents do not experience the uneasiness of the Traditionals or the anxiety of the Separates before arguments. Yet as they retroactively replay a prior argument in their minds, they relive the intensity of the emotions felt during the argument. Because Independents verbalize conflict, IIs linked to these arguments enable them to examine their disagreements and enhance their chances of working through them. Thus, the self-understanding function discussed in chapter 3 appears to be more applicable to the Independents when thinking about arguments compared with the Separates.

Traditionals reported less IIs about conflict than Independents and Separates. Even when they imagine arguments, they reported less emotional intensity. For this couple type, IIs about arguing are helpful. Self-understanding and rehearsal are used as they plan and review what they say to each other. Gendrin and Werner (1996-1997) concluded that thinking about serious issues toward satisfactory conclusions enhances the cooperation and conciliation typical of traditional couples.

HAVING IIS WITH INCOMPETENT TEACHERS

Berkos (1999) studied a major area in which conflict is kept alive: having IIs with a teacher who is aggressive, arrogant, harassing, or incompetent. Teachers hold power over students by virtue of being able to dispense grades. Kearney et al. (1991) defined teacher misbehaviors as behaviors that interfere with instruction and learning.

Incompetent teachers demonstrate the following behaviors: confusing/unclear lectures, apathy to students, unfair testing, boring lectures, information overload, not knowing subject matter, foreign or regional accents, inappropriate volume, and bad grammar/spelling. The profiles of incompetent teachers are those who assign excessive work and rush though information. Incompetent teachers may make exams too difficult, discourage student input, and generally seem to lack personal affect for the students or the course. They are likely to deliver boring lectures and rely on a monotone voice or inappropriate volume (Kearney et al., 1991).

Offensive teachers use six teacher misbehaviors: sarcasm/putdowns, verbal abuse, unreasonable/arbitrary rules, sexual harassment, negative personality, and favoritism/prejudice. Offensive teachers may embarrass or demean the students while being considered chauvinistic or playing favorites. They may use profanity, insult students, and talk about topics inappropriate for classroom discussion (Kearney et al., 1991). Students may find offensive teachers rude and egotistical.

Finally, indolent teachers are absent, tardy, and unprepared/disorganized; deviate from syllabus; return work late, and do not challenge the students by not giving enough information. Indolent teachers are likely to be disorganized and late to class. They may fall behind the course schedule and forget to collect and return homework assignments. Typically, indolent teachers make their classes too easy and fail to provide their students with enough information, challenge, or learning opportunities.

Berkos (1999) surveyed 237 university students ages 18 to 50 (averaged 20.3 years) from a variety of backgrounds (e.g., Asian American, White, Latino, African American, Native American). The students read a paragraph describing one of three types of teacher misbehaviors (incompetent, offensive, or indolent) with examples of the targeted teacher type. They were asked how likely they would have IIs with the targeted teacher. Actual communication was measured by asking the students how likely they would be to actually interact with an incompetent (or offensive or indolent) teacher like the one described in the profile and if they would confront the teacher.

Students indicated that they would be likely to use IIs with a misbehaving teacher. However, when asked if they would actually confront the teacher, most students did not. When teachers misbehave, students are still keeping conflict alive intrapersonally, even when they do not confront the teacher. Berkos (1999) found that students with an offensive teacher had more IIs than students thinking about an indolent or incompetent teacher.

Berkos (1999) speculated that the offensive teacher causes the most emotional response. This results in II usage because the offensive teacher is most in violation of students' expectancies for their teacher. The negative expectancy violation causes a greater need for IIs. Indolent misbehaviors may involve fewer emotional responses because the misbehaviors are less personal in nature. Berkos (1999) also speculated that the lower frequency of IIs with the indolent teacher when compared with the offensive teacher could be that students identify more with the indolent teacher than the offensive teacher. According to attribution theory, students would see indolent misbehaviors as more forgivable than offensive misbehaviors, because the students engage in indolent type behaviors, such as tardiness and not delivering prompt assignments.

SUMMARY

Imagined interactions keep conflict alive as well as reduce it. Individuals link a series of arguments together by replaying old conversations in their minds while rehearsing for anticipating encounters. Old memories may fester inside because there are symbols in the environment that reminds us of old arguments. II conflict linkage theory is designed to explain why conflict is maintained. A series of axioms and theorems reflects the endurance of conflict.

Current moods affect the valence of IIs in terms of how positive or negative imagined interactions are. Hence, thinking about positive outcomes is beneficial in resolving conflict. This is discussed in more detail in the next chapter. Despite the power of positive thinking, when an individual attempts to think only positive thoughts, negative IIs will sometimes intrude on the positive feelings. Keeping conflict alive also has the potential to distort reality because thinking about conflict facilitates anticipating messages that may be discrepant from what actually occurs.

People use IIs as a mechanism to escape from societal norms. An individual can imagine letting off steam in an II with a person in a managerial position while never actually communicating the message. Two functions are served: catharsis and compensation.

The themes of personal relationships are revealed through analysis of the topics of IIs with relational partners. For example, there are conflict themes reflecting personalities, behaviors of the interaction partners, and norms in terms of the partner following implicit rules for the role he or she occupies (e.g., "Don't raise your voice, when arguing with me," "Respect my opinion").

Research reveals that married couples who have the Separatist orientation are not able to constructively think of arguments before arguments. In contrast, Traditionals and Independents are more likely to imagine productive outcomes when thinking about arguing with their partners over some issue.

Conflict is kept alive when dealing with teacher misbehaviors. University students report more IIs when thinking about an offensive teacher who ridicules students while showing favoritism toward others than incompetent teachers who do not know the subject matter that well or indolent teachers who are lazy. Unfortunately, conflict is kept alive partially because the teacher–student relationship resembles a supervisor–subordinate relationship when there are power differences. Unless the student actually confronts the teacher or the teacher's department chair, students may cope intrapersonally with teacher misbehaviors through IIs that serve the catharsis function.

Chapter 6

CROSS-CULTURAL COMPARISONS

OF IIs

Imagined interactions have been studied in terms of the characteristics and functional differences across different cultures. Krober and Kluckhohn (1952) reviewed 164 definitions of culture and summarized them in terms of the following definition:

> Culture consists of pattern, explicit and implicit, of and for behavior acquired and transmitted by symbols, constituting the distinctive achievements of human groups, including their embodiments in artifacts; the essential core of culture consists of traditional ideas and their attached value. (p. 181)

Culture perpetuates itself to the extent that it conditions people and, in turn, is conditioned by the beliefs and action of individuals (Singelis & Brown, 1995). Culture provides the guidance and rewards that shape individuals' self-concepts. Yet culture is perpetuated and modified by the actions of its members. Shweder (1979) discussed how culture influences self-concept in terms of how individuals view themselves in relation to others. Singelis and Brown (1995) argued how culture affects an individual's definition of the self and importance of espousing certain values (e.g., self-gain vs. helping others), which in turn affects communication behavior.

A mechanism shaping an individual's self-image to their manifestation of communication behaviors is IIs. In this chapter, a number of studies

91

examining IIs across different cultures are reviewed. First, independence and interdependence are examined in terms of self-concept. Second, four different cultural patterns are reviewed: horizontal individualism, horizontal collectivism, vertical individualism, and vertical collectivism. Subsequently, IIs in the Pacific Rim are examined. IIs among foreigners temporarily residing in the United States are examined as well as college students from China preparing to come over to the United States. Finally, an analysis of IIs used by Chinese students before and after a demonstration in Beijing, China that concerned student demands for more democracy is discussed.

INDEPENDENT VERSUS INTERDEPENDENT CONCEPTIONS OF SELF

Western countries such as the United States have an independent view of the self that emphasizes the uniqueness of individuals and sees that the self is autonomous and independent. In contrast, Markus and Kitayama (1991) discussed an interdependent or collective self-concept in which non-Western countries such as Japan stress relationships, connection with others, and putting the needs of others before the needs of the self. Singelis and Brown (1995) discussed how individuals may endorse both individualism and collectivism depending on how the culture encourages the development of an interdependent or independent self. Yet the self can be viewed as an adaptive mechanism for navigating the social environment (Markus & Kitayama, 1994). People vary in the extent to which they follow cultural mandates.

Individualists are direct in their speeches, are spontaneous, have personal verbal styles, focus on personal identity, move easily between groups, and show emotions (Singelis, 1994a). Conversely, collectivists are indirect in their speech, are intuitive, have a contextual verbal style, focus on role identity, have more difficulty moving between groups, and restrict display of emotions. Collectivists are polite, indirect, and nonverbal, which facilitates maintaining harmonious relationships (Singelis, 1994a). In managing conflict, collectivists prefer indirect forms of speech such as keeping silent, apologizing, expressing their feelings to a third party, and being passive. In fact, Ueda (1974) identified 16 ways that the Japanese avoid saying "no." For example, Japanese may hesitate or say something ambiguous as an indirect way of saying no or when they believe what they would directly say could be disagreeable to others (Doi, 1973). Koreans prefer hinting as a form of request, whereas Americans prefer asking directly for something (M. Kim, 1993).

Speaking and self-expression are necessary communication skills for individualists who move easily between groups. Conversely, empathy is more critical for collectivists who are socialized by the culture to listen and spend more time in smaller groups of people who less often express themselves directly.

Singelis (1994) reviewed research indicating that Japanese and Korean mothers engaged in empathy training for listening skills with their 2-year-olds. Tobin, Wu, and Davidson (1989) reported how in China there is encouragement of memorization, diction, self-confidence, and enunciation, whereas Americans encourage speaking up, asking questions, and expressing opinions.

In terms of roles, collectivists are guided by hierarchical role systems that promote harmony and solidarity by clearly designating leadership while group members have an accepted place in the group. Individualists attempt to minimize role differences to protect their independence and privacy (Singelis, 1994). When thinking about themselves, individualists are likely to refer to their own abilities, personal attributes, or goals. Collectivists refer to the feelings, thoughts, or actions of others. Relationships are of great importance, and even if the costs outweigh the rewards, collectivists tend to stay in the relationships (Kim, Triandis, Kagitcibasi, & Yoon, 1994). Social behavior with collectivists is predicted from norms, whereas among individualists behavior is predicted from attitudes.

Finally, collectivists have personal goals that overlap with the goals of groups of which they are members. If there is a discrepancy between individual and group goals, group goals take precedence. Conversely, individualists have personal goals that may or may not overlap with group goals. If there is a discrepancy between the two levels of goals, individualists believe their personal goals should have priority over the group (Schwartz, 1990).

Singelis and Brown (1995) discussed how individualism and collectivism coexist within people. Yet the varying emphasis that pervades these two types of culture rewards the development of a collective or individualistic self. Modern, industrial-urban, fast-changing cultures tend to be individualistic, whereas agricultural, static cultures are collectivist. Despite the rewards of the culture, the self is viewed as an adaptive mechanism for navigating the social environment (Markus & Kitayama, 1994). Because of their co-existence within individuals, individuals vary in the amount they internalize either collectivism or individualism. Furthermore, economic distinctions affect these beliefs. Within both collectivist and individualistic cultures, the upper classes tend to be individualist, whereas the lower and middle classes are more collectivist (Singelis, Triandis, Bhawuk, & Gelfand, 1995).

Individualism may be associated with self-dominant IIs. Because the expression of ideas is encouraged in individualistic self-concepts, more attention could be concentrated on one's own messages. Yet it can also be argued that the emphasis on listening in collectivist cultures may be associated with the simple activity of having IIs. Self-dominant IIs may be less in collectivist cultures.

Before discussing this in further detail, it is helpful to delineate individualism and collectivism based on distinctions between horizontal and vertical dimensions of self-construal resulting in four types of selves. As noted previously, collectivism and individualism co-exist within people. Triandis

(1995) discussed how some individualists including Americans associate self-reliance with competition, whereas others do not. Some collectivists including the Japanese emphasize in-group harmony, whereas others do not. For example, East Asians would rather deceive another to save face and avoid confrontation, whereas the Israeli Kibbutz have intense discussions resulting in people losing face even though both groups are collectivist.

CULTURAL PATTERNS OF HORIZONTAL/VERTICAL INDIVIDUALISM AND COLLECTIVISM

Horizontal Individualism

Horizontal individualism is a cultural pattern in which an autonomous self is important, but the self is more or less equal in status with others. This pattern is characteristic of Sweden and Australia (Daun, 1991). There is the desire to bring down those who have high status. Singelis and his associates (1995) characterized horizontal individualism as being independent, market pricing, high equality, high freedom, and democratic socialism. Horizontal individualists do their own thing, but do not necessarily compare themselves with others. Instead, they do not want to be distinguished (Triandis, Chen, & Chan, 1998).

Vertical Individualism

Vertical individualism is a cultural pattern in which the self is also important, yet individuals view others as different. Competition characterizes social relations. There are differences in authority based on status, low equality, high freedom, and a market democracy (Singelis et al., 1995). Self-reliance is stressed, and being *Number One* is important. Vertical individualists are insulted if it is suggested to them that they are *average* (Weldon, 1984). There is authority ranking, market pricing, high freedom, and market democracy. Vertical individualists are concerned with being compared to others and want to be distinguished for their uniqueness (Triandis et al., 1998). The United States and France are examples of this cultural pattern as are the middle and upper classes in many Western democracies and in the United States.

Horizontal Collectivism

Singelis and his colleagues (1995) defined *horizontal collectivism* as a cultural pattern in which the individual views the self as part of an in-group to the extent that the self is merged with other members of the in-group, all of whom are similar to each other. Horizontal collectivists merge with in-groups (e.g., family, coworkers, and neighbors), but do not feel subordinate to the in-groups (Triandis, Chen, & Chan, 1998). Equality symbolizes horizontal collectivism. Horizontal collectivists are interdependent, desire equality matching, have lower freedom, and value communal living. The Israeli Kibbutz is an example of this cultural pattern. An extreme example of this pattern given by Singelis and his associates (1995) is theoretical communism.

Vertical Collectivism

Vertical collectivism is a cultural pattern in which members of the in-group have status differences. Although the self is interdependent with other in-group members, inequality is accepted and people are not viewed as being the same. Vertical collectivism is characterized by interdependence, authority ranking, low equality, low freedom, and communalism. Another important characteristic of vertical collectivism is that serving and sacrificing for the in-group is expected (Singelis et al., 1995). Vertical collectivists submit to the norms of their in-groups. Rural villages in India are examples of this cultural pattern. An extreme example of this pattern was Nazi Germany.

IIS IN THE PACIFIC RIM

The relationship between cultural patterns and imagined interactions has been examined among college students in California, Thailand, and Japan. Honeycutt and McCann (2001) surveyed 484 college students ranging in age from 18 to 63 that consisted of the following percentages in the sample: Americans (41%), Thais (31%), and Japanese (28%). Horizontal and vertical dimensions of individualism and collectivism were measured using a 32-item scale developed by Singelis et al. (1995). Americans were highest in horizontal individualism followed by Japanese and Thais in descending order (Honeycutt & McCann, 2001). Both Americans and Japanese were higher in horizontal collectivism than the Thais. In addition, Japanese were highest in vertical collectivism followed by Americans and Thais in descending order.

    The characteristics and functions of imagined interactions were measured using a modified version of the SII developed by Honeycutt et al. (1992-1993). New items were written for conflict linkage, other dominance, and imagining what one could say if societal norms allowed it.

    Recall from chapter 5, that II conflict linkage theory explains why conflict endures, how it is maintained, why it may be constructive or destructive, and how it can erupt at any point during interpersonal communication. Theorem 2 states: The current mood and emotional state of individuals is associated with whether their IIs are positive or negative. The better a person's mood, the more positive his or her IIs will be as well as the inverse.

Honeycutt and McCann (2001) tested this theorem in their sample. They also measured other dominance. Other-dominance is when the self is in a listening role and imagines what the other might say. The ability to imagine what the other says involves perspective taking and empathy. They were interested in the Thai culture's emphasis on collectivism and how the self has not been taught to argue with others while deference is rewarded. They examined whether the Thais reported lower levels of self-dominance and higher levels of other-dominance in their IIs compared with Americans. They also examined Theorem 9: People use IIs as a mechanism for escape from societal norms. For example, people may be expected to talk a certain way with their bosses in real life, but in their IIs they can be considerably more bold or liberated. Other examples are speaking in any manner you desire because nobody has control over you and not feeling restricted by society's rules in your IIs.

Box 6.1 reflects a sample II journal report from a student whose parents were immigrants from Japan. The student reports how conflict was maintained when discussing her sister's decision to live with a boyfriend, of whom the parents did not approve. Her account reflects the rehearsal function.

BOX 6.1

Journal Account of a Japanese Female Student Reporting on Conflict With Her Parents

Topic: Sister is living with her boyfriend

I talk to my parents about once a week in Japan. Before every conversation, I rehearse what I want to say. I prepare myself so I don't feel belittled by them. Our last conversation was about my sister. I knew what they were going to say and I was right. They complained about my sister planning to cohabitate with her boyfriend and they tried to get me to persuade her to change her mind. This is a very important issue in my family, and I really hope my sister is successful because she is paving the way for me.

In my II with my parents, I sounded very grown up and they treated me like a peer. I talked a lot and said things that I normally would not say. I told them they were old fashioned and that a lot of couples live together before marriage these days. My parents asked why not just get married instead of living in sin and have people criticize you behind your back? I told them the positive aspect of cohabitation—that couples get to know each other better to see if they are compatible for marriage when they live together to prevent divorce in the future.

In my II, I came up with a lot of good arguments, and my parents understood and listened. In my actual conversation with my parents, I repeated my arguments; however, they were not as understanding. They were angry that they raised two moralless daughters, but I was prepared for their arguments from my IIs. I told them just because some people look out for their future by cohabiting with a potential partner does not make them less moral, that in fact it is the responsible thing to do.

I believe my IIs with my parents helped me to have a productive conversation with them. By rehearsing what I wanted to say, I eliminated things that might have really offended my parents, resulting in them blocking me out completely. I think they really listened, even though they are not admitting that I said some good points.

I have a lot of IIs with the people I know. It wasn't until I learned about IIs that I realized how productive it is to think things over before the actual event. I think things over before the actual event. I now think becoming aware of IIs helps me be a better communicator.

Box 6.2 reveals additional associations among II characteristics, functions, and cultural patterns. The higher the coefficient, the more that the II characteristic or function predicted the cultural pattern in a positive or negative direction. For example, rehearsal was associated with both horizontal and vertical collectivism. Activity was associated with all cultural patterns except vertical individualism. Discrepancy was negatively associated with horizontal individualism, yet revealed a slight positive association with vertical individualism.

Self-dominance was associated with horizontal individualism and vertical individualism, in which the self imagines doing most of the talking. Hence, an individualist self-construal is characterized by thinking about messages in which the self does more talking while the other person(s) in the II listens. Conversely, as revealed in Box 6.2, other dominance was negatively associated with vertical individualism and vertical collectivism. Inequalities are expected in vertical patterns as opposed to horizontal patterns. A top-down hierarchy may promote imagery and thought that other individuals may take advantage of the self because competition is expected. Hence, attention is concentrated on one's own messages to justify one's own beliefs.

The idea of "think before you speak" is an American maxim that is reflected in having proactive IIs being associated with vertical individualism. Conversely, the lack of proactive IIs is related to horizontal individualism.

We are conducting additional II research among bilingual Chinese college students. The cultural patterns of horizontal/vertical collectivism and individualism may vary among bilingual or multilingual individuals depending on which language the person is using. For example, a Chinese student who is responding to descriptions of the cultural patterns while reading Chinese may think more collectively than when reading the descriptions in English.

BOX 6.2

Caption: II Predictors of Cultural Patterns

Cultural Pattern	II Characteristic or Function	Regression Coefficient
Vertical Individualism	Other dominance	-.21
	Self-dominance	.17
	Valence	.12
	Discrepancy	.09
	Proactivity	.10
Horizontal Collectivism	Proactivity	.10
	Self-understanding	.11
	Frequency	.16
	Conflict linkage	.11
	Rehearsal	.11
Vertical Collectivism	Other dominance	-.30
	Conflict linkage	.14
	Rehearsal	.11
	Self-dominance	.10
	Activity	.09

The theory of linguistic relativity, also known as the Sapir–Whorf hypothesis (Whorf, 1956), claims that language shapes our perceptions of reality and the environment. For example, Eskimos are more likely to notice and think about differences in snow than are native speakers of English who have only one term for snow (Cronkhite, 1976). Yet the theory is impossible to prove because we have no way to interpret reality without thinking thoughts expressed in language (Infante, Rancer, & Womack, 1997).

Indirect support for the hypothesis may be gathered by comparing how individuals respond to the cultural patterns and reports of IIs depending on which language they are using. A Chinese student may report more self-dominance when reporting IIs in English compared with reporting in Chinese. Similarly, higher levels of horizontal collectivism may be reported when reading about this description in Chinese than in English. Higher levels of vertical individualism may be reported by the Chinese students when reading the description in English than in Chinese.

AMERICAN, THAI, AND JAPANESE DIFFERENCES IN II CHARACTERISTICS

Honeycutt and McCann (2001) examined differences among Americans, Thais, and the Japanese. Box 6.3 contains the mean differences among Americans,

BOX 6.3

II Characteristics/Functions	Americans	Thais	Japanese	Significant Contrasts
Activity	5.18	4.74	5.01	A > T
Conflict linkage	3.60	4.31	5.17	J > T > A
Self-dominance	4.98	3.84	4.47	A > J > T
Other dominance	5.05	5.09	4.28	A, T > J
Boldness	4.77	4.74	5.38	J > A, T
Discrepancy	4.38	4.96	4.73	T, J > A
Variety	4.38	3.64	4.75	J > A > T
Specificity	4.87	4.03	4.26	A > T, J
Rehearsal	4.80	4.34	5.13	J > A > T
Self-understanding	4.60	4.36	5.13	J > A, T
Catharsis	4.63	4.18	5.01	J > T

Note. A = American, T = Thai, J = Japanese

Thais, and the Japanese on II characteristics and functions. As revealed in Box 6.3 Americans had the highest level of self-dominant IIs, whereas the Thais had the least, with Japanese in an intermediary position. In terms of other-dominant IIs, Americans and Thais had similar levels, whereas the Japanese were significantly lower. Americans had the most specific IIs.

The Japanese had the highest levels of conflict linkage, boldness, variety, rehearsal, self-understanding, and catharsis. The Thais were low on a number of dimensions including activity, self-dominance, boldness, variety, rehearsal, self-understanding, and catharsis. The only characteristic that characterized Thais more than Americans was discrepancy.

The II profile of an American is an individual who is less likely to maintain thoughts about conflict, but is dominant in their IIs and has specific IIs. The Thais have discrepant IIs with less rehearsal and fewer interaction partners. Conversely, the Japanese are emboldened in their IIs, have a variety of interaction partners, and keep conflict alive.

Conflict linkage was associated with horizontal collectivism and vertical collectivism. In collectivism, concern for others is important as opposed to solely concentrating on self-needs. There may be more forgiveness. Forgiveness occurs when individuals do not want to avoid the offender and see harm coming to the offending partner (McCullough et al., 1998). Forgiving is associated with a willingness to sacrifice for the relationship, empathy, judgments of blame, lack of rumination, perceived intentionality, severity, and avoidability of the offense (Boon & Sulsky, 1997; Girard & Mullet, 1997). Conversely, revenge is associated with rumination and dwelling on negative thoughts (McCullough et al., 1998). Conflict linkage is rumination about negative affect. In collectivist cultures, there may be a maxim operating of "forgive, but do not forget," whereas in individualistic cultures, there is less negative rumination. Indeed, competition may foster the idea of getting over it and proceeding ahead to other areas.

Americans were characterized by being talkative and specific in their IIs, yet ruminating less about conflict. The Japanese were more likely to ruminate over conflict, have a variety of II topics/partners, and be more emboldened in their IIs. The Thais were characterized by having more discrepant IIs, yet less activity, variety, rehearsal, and catharsis. As noted earlier, Americans were highest in horizontal individualism. Triandis (1995) suggested that the United States was an example of this pattern. Yet horizontal individualism is a cultural pattern where the individual is more or less equal in status with others while satisfaction of autonomous needs is expected. The American dream of achieving goals and wealth without being restricted by race or gender reflects the ideal of horizontal individualism. Furthermore, individuals vary in their endorsement of these patterns and, in fact, can endorse combinations of the patterns (Singelis & Brown, 1995).

FUNCTIONS OF IIS AMONG TEMPORARY SOJOURNERS VISITING AMERICA

Gendrin (1991) discussed *cross-cultural adaptation* among temporary sojourners. Cross-cultural adaptation is defined as a process of change that takes place intrapersonally as individuals come into prolonged first-hand contact with a new culture (Kim, 1988). Temporary sojourners are individuals who are temporarily residing in a foreign country. Because they return to their homeland, they are less committed to becoming full members of the host society. According to Furnham (1987), a sojourner tends to stay from 6 months to 5 years at a place with the intent to return home. Foreign students, as representatives of sojourners, report living abroad to get a degree or professional training (Klineberg & Hull, 1979). As sojourners enter a different culture, they go through an adaptation process called *acculturation*. Acculturation is defined as "culture change that results from continuous, firsthand contact between two distinct cultural groups" (Berry, Kim, & Boski, 1987, p. 64).

Sojourners are further characterized by integration. According to Berry (1984), *integration* involves having the individual establish relationships within the host culture while maintaining his or her cultural identity. Integration can be contrasted with assimilation, which involves relinquishing one's cultural identity while maintaining relationships with other groups. Temporary sojourners do not want to change their cultural identity while establishing significant relationships with other groups. Hence, it also is assumed that they strategize for positive encounters to function properly in the host culture. They can use IIs to rehearse for anticipated encounters with members of the host culture. Gendrin (1991) discussed how temporary sojourners must test their interpretations and cognitive representations of their own and the host cultures. They must review their own communication and individuals in the host culture to learn and adapt.

IIs provide a mechanism by which temporary sojourners may access information to make sense of their cross-cultural experience. Yet Gendrin (1991) also discussed how IIs may be dysfunctional when sojourners have not developed the "appropriate, emotional, and physical responses to the new cultural milieu" (p. 132). She discussed how sojourners in the initial stage of adaptation may rely on cognitive representations that are incompatible with their cross-cultural experiences because they may recall experiences from their homeland that may not explain current activities. Gendrin (1991) reported how sojourners frequently have IIs to evaluate their experiences and develop a behavioral script that will be effective in the host culture. She found that international students imagined themselves conversing in English with classmates, professors, and landlords. The topics of their IIs focused on academic and social events. They discussed grades, course assignments, and rent.

Temporary sojourners are filled with a lot of anxiety and uncertainty as they enter the host culture. Gudykunst (1988) discussed how temporary sojourners are not sure how to behave and experience greater uncertainty than members of the host culture. Initially, they rely on an implicit theory of their own culture to guide their behavior and interpret the behavior of host nationals. Temporary sojourners rehearse anticipated encounters with members of the host culture to reduce uncertainty and enhance their integration into the host culture. They also use retroactive IIs as a basis to evaluate and develop effective behaviors.

Gendrin (1991) also discussed how the interaction partners in IIs should vary. Foreign students tend to belong to three social networks with varying importance. The first network consists of co-nationals who provide opportunities for sojourners to rehearse and express their culture of origin. The second network consists of ties with important host nationals including academics, landlords, student advisers, and government officials. The third network consists of host national friends (Furnham & Alibhai, 1985). Temporary sojourners' IIs are with these individuals. Yet, Gendrin (1991) indicated that sojourners who have IIs with individuals of the host culture are more likely to quickly adapt compared with those who imagine conversing with ethnic nationals.

USING IIS TO LEARN ENGLISH AS A SECOND LANGUAGE

Gendrin (1992) examined international students learning English as a second language. Studies in second language acquisition support the notion that learning a second language involves active processes that are cognitive and social in nature (O'Malley & Chamot, 1999). These strategies have been identified in structured environments such as foreign language classrooms. Yet when foreign students do not learn the host language in the classroom, they rely on non-classroom settings to practice the host language. The cognitive processing of the host language can be studied in terms of imagined interactions. IIs are a cognitive process by which foreign nationals can achieve competence in the host language.

In learning a second language, the concept of *declarative knowledge* refers to knowledge of syntax and noun–verb placement. Declarative knowledge includes definitions of words, facts, and rules about language. Procedural knowledge reflects knowledge about how to speak. According to Anderson's (1980) theory of language learning, declarative knowledge consists of the formal rules of language. In a foreign language classroom, the language is learned by using general rule-following procedures (i.e., add an "s" to generate the plural of a noun when the noun ends in a hard consonant), rather than speaking directly as in the native language. However, not all the rules that speakers use in second language acquisition are learned in foreign language classrooms. According to O'Malley and Chamot (1999), individuals generate their own rules for using language depending on the rule's utility in helping the individual achieve linguistic competence. Considering that foreign nationals frequently imagine conversations with host nationals, their IIs become the linguistic data they use to uncover the rules for second language competence. Indeed, IIs contribute to the development, storage, and retrieval of knowledge that individuals use to uncover the rules for a given language. These rules do not always reflect the formal rules of the target language but are ad hoc rules that clarify for non-native speakers what works in a given conversation.

Grounded in actual conversations, IIs not only serve to develop a declarative knowledge of a second language, but also help develop rules for communication competence in the second language (Gendrin, 2000a). IIs may bring to non-native speakers' awareness rules of syntax, discourse, semantics, and phonology. As non-native speakers imagine a conversation with native speakers, they anticipate what they might say in the target language using the rehearsal function of IIs. After a given encounter has failed, non-native speakers may review in their mind what happened to determine which rule of discourse they violated. Consequently, they may plan a new production strategy by choosing from alternative ones or ask a native speaker for clarification or correction. Hence, engaging in proactive and retroactive IIs in the target language may facilitate non-native speakers' learning of the rules of the second language.

When non-native speakers imagine themselves talking with native speakers, they may use scripted or partially scripted lines of dialogue that reflect rules of discourse from their native language. Although not necessarily effective initially, using a script in the target language through an II may facilitate the construction of new scripts in the second language.

IIS AND STAGES OF LANGUAGE ACQUISTION

Gendrin (2000a) discussed the role of IIs in acquiring second language skills in three stages. The first stage is the cognitive stage, which involves a conscious mental activity on the part of second language learners to understand what is being said in the second language. Hence, second language learners develop declarative knowledge. For example, Krashen and Scarcella (1978) argued that in order to meet conversational demands, second language learners could memorize and use appropriate whole utterances and phrases without understanding their internal structure. Gendrin (2000a) cited Ventrigla (1982), who used the example of a second language learner who could use the expression *HeygimmmedebalY* and identify the similarity with *Heygimmidepencil* without being aware of its grammatical component parts. The beginning learners could have used IIs in the second language to reconstruct entire phrases and sentences that may help them achieve specific communication outcomes. This mental rehearsal of short interactional lines require beginning learners to focus their attention on what is being said to remember entire utterances. This, in turn, would indicate that beginning learners' IIs focus on the other person and not on themselves. Gendrin (2000a) discussed how the language learners pay careful attention to how a native speaker sounds in an attempt to replicate the proper pronunciation. Thus, second language learners' IIs would be other oriented as opposed to imagining themselves uttering lines of dialogue. As second language learners become more proficient in the second language, their IIs may shift to the self talking more than the other as they try to produce words that are more congruent with utterances in the target language. Gendrin (2000a) believes that their IIs are likely to be more self-oriented where they dominate the conversation. Yet the IIs function differentially as second language learners move from the cognitive stage of learning to the next stage.

The second stage of language acquisition is the association stage. Anderson (1980, 1983) discussed how second language learners fine tune their declarative knowledge of the target language by uncovering the procedures necessary for competent communication in that language. O'Malley and Chamot (1999) characterized this stage, whereby second language learners gradually correct language errors as they become more proficient at detecting discrepancies between their production skills and the utterances they receive. IIs used retroactively and proactively would help in this stage.

The final stage of second language acquisition is the autonomous stage. In this last stage, second language learners automatically process the language for functional purposes, whether it is to achieve social, academic, or technical goals. Gendrin's (1991) findings provide some evidence of the autonomous processing of language through IIs. When testing for a variety of II characteristics, international students reported having IIs in English with American classmates, university professors, and landlords. The conversations imagined focused on social as well as academic activities and assignments.

Gendrin (1992, 2000a) also discussed three types of learning strategies that non-native speakers use to acquire a second language. Metacognitive strategies involve planning for written or oral discourse, monitoring comprehension or production of statements, and evaluating language comprehension or production. Cognitive strategies affect incoming information directly and include the rehearsal, organization, elaboration of information, and use of verbal or visual imagery to understand and remember statements. Finally, social/affective strategies involve interacting with another person, asking for clarification, and engaging in IIs to reduce anxiety about a task (O'Malley & Chamot, 1999).

Gendrin (1992) discussed a number of advantages in viewing IIs as a cognitive strategy for learning a second language. First, it represents a type of mental process for acquiring a second language that is grounded in everyday conversations between non-native and native speakers. Second, this mental process is natural because it takes place in an authentic language context outside of formal classrooms. Therefore, it has the characteristics of actual discourse in the second language. Unfortunately, most cognitive strategies have been identified in a formal classroom setting. Little thought has been given to second language learning strategies in informal contexts.

IIS AMONG CHINESE STUDENTS PREPARING TO STUDY IN THE UNITED STATES

Petress (1995) interviewed 56 students in China preparing to study in the United States about their IIs. They ranged in age from 21 to 31 (mean age = 24.2). The students were preparing for graduate study at the master's (45%) and doctoral levels (55%). A variety of academic fields were represented including physics, engineering, computer science, biology, language, social sciences, humanities, and the arts.

The Chinese students reported having IIs in three settings: (a) interviews with others connected with their foreign study plans, (b) reviewing and evaluating each interview after it occurred, and (c) rehearsing future meetings with a major professor. The IIs specifically occurred with Chinese academic advisors, other Chinese school officials, the future American advisor, and family members. More than two thirds of the Chinese students reported that the rehearsal function of IIs was helpful in message planning.

TOPICS OF IIS

Three topics dominated the IIs of the Chinese students. The most frequently mentioned topic (29%) was the need for students to be aware of domestic and foreign political concerns. Second, was an explicit assurance that the student would return to China promptly after the graduate program was finished (27%). The third most popular topic was the student's desire to conduct research (17%). Other topics included the student's fitness for foreign study, arrangements for the impending separation, and need for summer employment.

Petress (1995) noted a gender difference in the topics. Men comprised 75% of the topics about political awareness and 91% of responses about promptly returning to China after their graduate study was finished. He noted that historically men in China have been monitored for weekly or biweekly political indoctrination classes. Men are frequently punished for failure to attend political classes. The Chinese women II topics were concerned with fitness for foreign study, impending separation from China, and need for summer employment. According to Petress, these topics deal with self-concept, ties to family/friends, and security.

ADDITIONAL GENDER DIFFERENCES

A variety of additional gender differences were observed. Two thirds of the Chinese female students reported that rehearsing their IIs was helpful for what actually happened in later real conversations. Half of the men reported their IIs to have a neutral affect on future interactions. This may be related to Chinese male students also focusing more imagery on their own messages, compared with Chinese female students who focused on both their own messages as well as the interaction partner's statements in their IIs. Men reported directness and brevity as a heuristic use of their IIs. Women reported that they needed to be more assertive. Chinese men also reported longer IIs, some lasting up to an hour longer than women. Petress (1995) indicated that the longer II duration by men could reflect a subtle argument strategy observed among Chinese men. Chinese women seem less inclined to qualify or contextualize their needs than Chinese men. Confidence building was a major issue reported by the Chinese females. Insofar as rehearsing conversations with their future advisors, Chinese males were more likely to use Chinese in their IIs (92%), whereas 41% of the Chinese female students reported using both English and Chinese and 59% of the females reported English as their II language.

A CASE STUDY OF IIS CONCERNING THE TIAN-AN-MEN SQUARE STUDENT DEMONSTRATION IN CHINA

Petress (1990) also reported on a case study among Chinese students in Beijing, China following the 1989 Tian-an-men Square student demonstrations. Hu Yao Bang, a deposed Chinese official who had supported students' rights to demonstrate, died in April 1989. His death invited an outpouring of mourning. The celebration of that grief took the form of a wreath laying in Tian-an-men Square, the seat of Chinese government, where an earlier Hu-supported demonstration had been violently crushed by the Chinese army. Chinese leaders, fearing an uncontrollable riot at the state funeral, planned prohibiting students from attending the ceremony in Hu's honor. This plan was leaked to foreign press reporters, and students made their way to the Square before they could be blocked from entering by the Chinese Army.

Government leaders began envisioning student democracy as seeds of rebellion and the first step in an attempt to overthrow the government. Government officials were upset by the foreign press coverage that the students enjoyed and by the horrible image that the coverage portrayed of the government. Using Bormann's (1985) symbolic convergence theory and fantasy theme analysis, Petress (1990) analyzed IIs in relation to the fantasies that the students had about their government. Bormann believed that the media had the power to dramatize and focus an event to cause fantasies to chain out through numerous demonstrators.

Bales (1970) analyzed group fantasies as a type of communication that occurs in small groups through the telling of stories. Bormann (1985) extended Bales' notion of storytelling into symbolic convergence theory. This theory argues that communication creates reality, symbols create reality for individuals, and the meaning of the symbols can converge among a group of individuals to create a shared reality for participants in the group. Various groups in the 1989 Tian-an-men demonstration generated fantasy themes out of their aspirations, hopes, fears, and experiences.

Petress (1990) discovered that two major visions emerged from the interviews he had with the students about Tian-an-men Square. The first fantasy involved an unchanged China that was rigid and would not hesitate to use lethal force to enforce its demands. The second vision envisioned a country that would change and be more democratic, liberal, and tolerant than were previous dynasties.

Petress discussed how student demonstration leaders requested a meeting with government leaders to discuss their freedom demands and that official corruption be investigated and reduced. Initially, this request was ignored; however, the foreign press convinced government leaders that it would be in the government's public relations interest to meet with the student leaders. A meeting between limited numbers of student leaders and the government was set to be televised over live Chinese TV.

Several students involved in the meeting and its planning reported having IIs that served the rehearsal function. They rehearsed anticipated questions and optimally corresponding answers. They even had group sessions to practice questions and answers. Hence, there was a collective II within the groups. The students reported that, after a while, the distinction between their own individual IIs and the group verbalized sessions was blurred.

Unfortunately, there was moderate discrepancy in the group IIs. The meeting with government leaders, although symbolically a victory for the students, resulted in few gains in their struggle for more democracy. Some student leaders imagined that the government officials would reason and compromise, which did not happen. Yet discrepancy was evident when the Chinese demonstrators imagined that many of their questions and answers with the government officials would be fresh and spontaneous. Instead, they also relied on the group-rehearsed II as did government officials.

Petress (1990) reported on some of the more poignant topics and interaction partners of the students' IIs. These included conversations with parents and teachers about the motivation for protesting should they survive the impending government attack. Other conversations involved pleas on behalf of comrades should they be injured, how to tell comrades' families should their friends be killed or injured, and how to find friends with ways to leave China should they become fortunate enough to survive what was ahead.

In terms of proactive IIs and rehearsing for anticipated interrogations, several Chinese students studying in the United States at the time of the demonstration believed that they would be interrogated by Chinese officials when they returned to their homeland. The official assumption may be that any Chinese student in the United States at the time of the uprising is suspected of aiding the student cause. Petress (1990) reported that the students were preparing mental scripts—responses to questions and accusations of whether they were actually guilty of tangible or emotional support to the students' cause. Some Chinese students who were pursuing graduate study in psychology described their concern that these scripts were constructed as defense mechanisms for a hostile audience, yet interfere with the uninhibited flow of honest expressions of their beliefs, feelings, and goals later when such discussions could take place without fear.

SUMMARY

Individuals from different countries reveal that IIs are endemic across cultures. Cross-cultural comparisons of II characteristics reveal similarities among Americans, Japanese, Thais, and Chinese. Americans have more self-dominant IIs, which reflects an individualistic orientation. Differences between horizontal and vertical collectivism and individualism were discussed. While members of a given culture vary in the extent to which they endorse these dimensions, they primarily lean to these orientations as a function of socialization within their culture. For example, Americans are high on vertical individualism, in which the individual, autonomous needs are stressed, yet differences are recognized from top to bottom in terms of socioeconomic success.

Temporary sojourners are individuals from another country who are staying in a foreign country for a fixed time and return to their native culture. Their IIs involve both English and their native language. Learning a second language involves the rehearsal function of IIs. Foreign nationals have IIs in their native language and learn the rules for the second language through imagining conversations with the speakers in the second language.

Chapter 7

IIs in an Assortment

of Contexts

This chapter discusses IIs in a variety of contexts and situations. Cancer may be a fatal condition in which individuals prepare to die. Research was done at a cancer clinic in which terminally ill patients were interviewed about their IIs with their physicians. The next section discusses whether IIs can occur with deceased loved ones. For example, the cancer patient who just dies may be in the minds of his or her loved ones. They may remember old sayings or messages from the just departed. IIs may be part of the bereavement process as individuals manage through grief and move forward in stages of growth and coping. Next, IIs among forensic competitors and debaters are examined in terms of coaching strategies for success.

IIs in the business organization are examined. A study by some of my graduate students examined the rehearsal function among banking executives as well as how often they had IIs in terms of frequency. Next is a discussion about the relationship between telling lies in terms of being deceptive and the function of IIs among those who are being deceptive. The chapter ends with a brief discussion of the relationship between IIs and prayer. In this regard, do individuals who pray often also have recurring IIs? What is the function of prayer in relation to IIs?

TERMINAL CANCER PATIENTS AND IIS WITH PHYSICIANS

According to the American Cancer Society (2000), the National Center Institute estimates that approximately 8.4 million Americans alive today have a history of cancer. More than 1,500 people die of cancer every day. Cancer is the second leading cause of death in the United States, exceeded only by heart disease. Since 1990, approximately 13 million new cancer cases have been diagnosed. These estimates do not include noninvasive, basal, and skin cancers.

The psychological aspects of the disease have not been studied as extensively, although the emotional trauma resulting from cancer diagnosis and treatment can be great (Radley & Green, 1987). Greer, Moorey, and Watson (1989) reported that the way cancer patients cope with the psychological trauma affects their chances of long-term survival. For example, hopelessness and passivity are associated with poorer chances of recovery for women with breast cancer (Levy, Herberman, Malusih, Schlien, & Lippman, 1985). Klinger (1977) discussed how internal cognition is important in coping with crises. Although hopelessness and depression are common, a critical step toward recovery involves changing internal cognition from the crisis to productive thoughts of the future.

Gotcher and Edwards (1990) examined cancer patients' actual communication and IIs with health care professionals. For cancer patients, actual conversations and imagined interactions represent strategies for dealing with their cancer. Through actual interaction with health care professionals, family members, and friends, cancer patients acquire information and emotional support. Through IIs, cancer patients can enhance self-understanding of their plight, rehearse for actual communication with doctors, and express fears and hopes that they have been unable to display more openly. Gotcher and Edwards (1990) provided an example of a cancer patient who recalls interactions in which loved ones were informed about the cancer, rehearsing questions for their doctors, thinking of what to say if given a positive or negative prognosis, or even finding themselves spontaneously talking to the cancer. These IIs represent the catharsis function discussed in chapter 3, as well as creating scripts for actual interaction and for dealing with the cancer. Gotcher and Edwards (1990) hypothesized that the frequency of actual communication about cancer would be positively associated with rehearsal and frequency of IIs as well as talking about fears being associated with pleasantness of IIs and catharsis.

They sampled 48 patients at a cancer treatment center whose average age was 62 years (ranged from 22 to 85). A modified version of the SII was used that included statements about their actual communication concerning cancer with health care professionals. Ninety-four percent of the patients reported having IIs about their cancer. Most were with doctors (48%), followed by spouses (22%) and other family members (13%). The topics of the IIs in descending order were cancer treatment (37%), the disease (17%), defeating the illness (14%), protecting the family from the illness (14%), and death (11%). In terms of emotional affect, a majority reported positive emotions (60%), with only 2% reporting negative feelings. Neutral (20%) and mixed (18%) affect comprised the other affective ratings.

The pleasantness of IIs was associated with using IIs for catharsis and imagining the self to be free of cancer. Using IIs for rehearsal was associated with the frequency of having them, catharsis, and imaging the self without cancer. The use of communication in reducing fear about the disease was associated with the catharsis function of IIs. Using communication to reduce fear was not associated with receiving emotional support from spouses. Cancer patients were reluctant to discuss their fears with their spouses. A number of patients reported that they had IIs attempting to protect their families from their own concern over their cancer. Although communication was associated with coping, some patients took a more passive approach in terms of trusting the physicians to make decisions and inform them about what they needed to know.

Consistent with prior research reviewed in chapter 2, Gotcher and Edwards (1990) found that the self talked more than the imagined interaction partner did. Yet for the individual with cancer, self-dominated IIs may reflect taking greater control and responsibility, leading to a more active role in actual conversations and better coping. Conversely, IIs dominated by an imagined interaction partner may reflect a more powerless attitude on the part of the patients, resulting in greater passivity in treatment.

Gotcher and Edwards (1990) found that rehearsal was related to actual communication about the cancer. Consequently, this was related to more productive coping. They provided an example of a man imagining telling his wife that he was dying. He imagined her responses and developed strategies for comforting her. However, for other patients, IIs could be dysfunctional for coping or recovery. Imagining the worst possible outcome may perpetuate hopelessness and depression and lead the patient to neglect treatment.

CAN WE HAVE IIS WITH DECEASED LOVED ONES?

People face various types and magnitudes of crises that can alter their lives dramatically. A major life event necessitating high levels of adjustment is the death of a loved one, especially when that loved one is the spouse (Gallegher, Thompson, & Peterson, 1981). Research suggests that the death of a spouse is a significant cause of stress that sometimes requires more readjustment than any other life event. Although various forms of bereavement and loss require adjustment, dealing with a spouse's death is cited as one of the most difficult forms of grief (Lowenstein, Landau, & Rosen, 1993).

One of the more challenging aspects of recovery for the surviving spouse is the disbanding of the spousal role (Farnsworth, Pett, & Lund, 1989).

Using symbolic interactionism as a conceptual framework, Farnsworth et al. (1989) discussed how widowhood represents major loss requiring an individual to define new roles consistent with his or her altered reality. This includes the disbanding of spousal roles. Prior to a spouse's death, the couple may have existed as a unit, with each member performing certain designated tasks as the *husband* or *wife*. Once one member of a couple is deceased, the remaining member is left to reorganize a life operated by a single individual rather than by a couple. This process is seemingly similar in the case of divorce. However, there are distinctions between psychosocial adjustments after divorce and bereavement.

Lopata (1973, 1975) discussed the identity reconstruction process that a surviving spouse experiences after the death of the partner. However, little has been offered to articulate the process that takes place to allow for such identity reconstruction. One possible means of tapping directly into the process of identity reconstruction and its mechanics is through the study of IIs. By analyzing the use of IIs by the surviving spouse, it is possible to examine the effects of communication on spousal bereavement and the contribution that intrapersonal communication processes such as IIs make to psychosocial adjustment to the death of a loved one.

Although role identity theory recognizes that identity adjustments do occur, it does not articulate how this process takes place. It seems quite likely that II usage allows a bereaved individual to transition from the spousal role identity to the widowed role identity by permitting one to visual the self interacting in the new role during the transition process. By examining IIs in relation to role identity theory, we can gain a greater understanding of how to comfort the bereaved as they transcend from old roles to new ones. For example, IIs may allow bereaved husbands or wives to transcend from the spousal role identity to the widowed role identity through verbal and visual imagery as discussed in chapter 1. Bereaved individuals can mentally envision their new role or rehearse being in the role of widow or widower. When one's spouse dies, the surviving spouse faces identity reformulation because the spousal role identity must then move out of the hierarchy, allowing for the integration of the widower or widow role identity. The reformulation of identity is facilitated by the use of IIs, whereas one's evaluation of success at such reformulation is facilitated by one's motivation and sense of personal control.

However, it is important to note that IIs with deceased loved ones reflect memories of the deceased. On the one hand, a retroactive II can occur with the deceased individual. Yet by definition a proactive II cannot occur with a deceased person because there will be no future face-to-face conversations with the person. Sometimes individuals are observed at gravesites talking to the deceased, but the deceased does not literally talk back. At best, individuals may spiritually or symbolically feel that the departed has *heard* what they said and *knows* what is going on. More research is needed in this area.

Lowenstein, Landau, and Rosen (1993) examined the impact of locus of control in aiding a widow during the adjustment phase. They found that belief in one's internal ability to control one's destiny, rather than an external orientation, which would have outside forces acting on the individual, was strongly associated with successful adjustment to a spouse's death. In their study, they examined adjustment consisting of four components: functioning in everyday living, depression level, health status, and life satisfaction. They found that the widow's perception of locus of control was strongly associated with all four components. Widows characterized by an internal locus of control were assessed as having adjusted better to the loss of their spouses than those with an external locus of control. Externally oriented widows reported poorer adjustment and were at a higher risk for needing further attention and assistance for dealing with the death of their spouses. However, understanding the process of identity reformulation by investigating the role of IIs can further our understanding of the role of communication and intrapersonal processes in the process of spousal bereavement.

IIS AMONG HOMELESS WOMEN

Gendrin (2000b) examined IIs in Louisiana among 75 residents of a women's shelter for homeless mothers. To stay at the shelter, one could not have a recent history of chemical dependency. The majority of the women were single, whereas others were divorced, separated, or widowed. The mothers had one or two children living with them in the shelter. Their educational levels ranged from sixth grade to 2 years of college. In fact, a number of the mothers had attended college.

Most of their IIs were with ex-relational partners, including husbands and boyfriends. Relationship topics dominated these IIs. Gendrin (2000b) speculated that the compensation function of IIs was operating because the IIs allowed a sense of social connectedness with those they were not seeing at the shelter. Some of the IIs reflected women's negative feelings about men, including this one with a roommate about alcohol abuse and sex:

— They want you to go out and drink with them, but don't get drunk. . . . If you get drunk, then you can't take care of them.
— But drunk enough to have sex.

Some of their IIs maintained conflict as discussed in chapter 5. For example, one mother imagined tell her abusive ex-husband: "Either be a father or a payment." She imagined him responding, "Go to hell! I won't do either." Gendrin (2000b) also gave an example of keeping conflict alive and fostering hatred in the following II:

— I hate you.

— I'd rather see you dead than free from me!

Aside from maintaining conflict, some of the IIs served the relationship maintenance function discussed in chapter 4. Following is an II with a roommate at the shelter about the man coming back:

— Why did he leave me?

— I don't know.

— I need a job and a better place to live and he might come back.

— Maybe.

— I wish he would come back.

Many of the homeless mothers' IIs were optimistic in terms of getting out of homelessness. The retroactive use of IIs allowed the homeless mothers to learn from prior experiences and rehearse for future encounters. Gendrin (2000b) noted that, "Thinking and talking internally about relationships allows homeless women to review or rewrite scripts for past and future conversations" (p. 215). Yet there was hope for the future. A number of the homeless mothers' IIs were concerned with getting a job, getting a house of their own, and moving on. Following is an example with a roommate:

— I want God to protect my children.

— Have no fear.

— I went job hunting today.

— Any luck?

— I turned in a couple of applications.

— Maybe they'll pan out.

It is interesting that many of the IIs were with roommates in the shelter. This supports Honeycutt's (1989b) findings that IIs often occur with individuals in close proximity to us as opposed to having numerous IIs with individuals we infrequently see. Recall from chapter 2 that Honeycutt (1989b) examined IIs among the elderly living in a retirement center. The residents reported having IIs with individuals living down in apartments near them. They had created new social families with fellow residents. Similarly, the mothers in the homeless shelter were having IIs with their newly created social families consisting of other residents or individuals that worked at the shelter.

Gendrin (2000b) reported that the homeless mothers' IIs reflected wishing for a better past or future and the pain of broken homes, addiction, and abuse. Thinking about the pain of the past is captured in the following sample II:

— Mom, I really miss my childhood.
— I understand, but you can't go back to that.
— But I want to.

The content of the homeless women's IIs revealed a life of continuity and change. Although the relationship was weak, Gendrin (2000b) found that the homeless women's level of satisfaction with their current relationships was positively related to overall life satisfaction.

Berg and Piner (1989) discussed how loneliness among homeless men is defined in terms of social isolation, whereas homeless women experience emotional isolation. It is interesting that the mothers did not report much loneliness. Prior studies on homelessness identified loneliness and a lack of social support as both a cause and effect of homelessness (e.g., Cohen & Wills, 1985; Crystal, 1984; Rook, 1988). Yet Gendrin (2000b) found that the women's overall level of loneliness was low. In fact, loneliness was only associated with having vague IIs. Honeycutt and his colleagues (1989-1990) also found this. As noted in chapter 2, they also found that loneliness was associated with having discrepant IIs that lacked a variety of topics and partners.

IIS IN FORENSIC COMPETITION

Forensics is an activity that requires participants to be aware of communication context. For example, debaters are rewarded by presenting good arguments, refuting opposing viewpoints, and responding to attacks about their own position. Debaters must adapt their messages to the judge. Individuals in prose, poetry, and dramatic interpretation are rewarded when they communicate empathy and understanding of textual concerns. Individuals in *after dinner speaking* are encouraged to *work* the audience and are rewarded for incorporating the peculiarities of the audience in their speech. In impromptu speaking, competitors are rewarded for generating fresh and intriguing insights on a quotation in less than 3 minutes. In platform speaking events, competitors are expected to appear spontaneous, although they may have repetitively delivered the same speech.

The selection of messages for forensic participants is in a constant process of evaluation and reevaluation. Debaters are required to choose from a repertoire of potential arguments to advance opposing arguments. They are required to engage in cross-examination, deal with exceptions to their arguments, and answer arguments that reflect the idiosyncrasies of the opposition.

The use of IIs may enhance forensic competitors' success. Using both visual and verbal imagery, IIs can enable forensic participants to mentally rehearse messages and prepare for possible exigencies. Gotcher and Honeycutt

(1989) sampled 73 individuals at three college tournaments. The individuals were relatively experienced at forensic competition, with more than 60% having forensic experience from 3 to 5 years. The sample consisted of individuals participating in debate (64%), individual events (26%), and both debate and individual competition (10%).

Gotcher and Honeycutt (1989) found that the IIs of debaters differed from those of individual event participants. The debaters had more IIs that were used for rehearsal compared with the individual event participants. Furthermore, most of their forensic IIs were with opponents as opposed to judges. Aside from opponents, popular II partners were teammates and coaches. Competitors who did well at the tournaments imagined success and positive outcomes in their IIs. Success in the IIs was correlated with having self-dominant IIs in terms of talking more than the opponent did and having proactive IIs before rounds. Actual success was negatively associated with discrepant IIs.

Gotcher and Honeycutt (1989) discussed how IIs could compensate for the lack of experience in the forensic activity. As the frequency of IIs increased for competitors, the discrepancy between imagined and real interactions decreased. Hence, as participants increased their awareness of the forensic activity through IIs or actual competition, their IIs mirrored reality more closely. Yet past success in forensic competition acts as a guide for future performances. Competitors repeat behaviors that were previously rewarded. IIs allow participants to rehearse behaviors and implement message strategies in subsequent competitions. The rehearsal function of IIs enables the inexperienced competitors to compensate for lack of experience by having IIs. Hence, in forensic competition, the rehearsal and compensation functions discussed in chapter 3 often are combined.

When competitors experienced IIs before the actual competition, they tended to report more success in the II. This finding reinforces the notion of a self-fulfilling prophecy. Before the competition, competitors imagined the best possible outcome. This result in conjunction with findings concerning discrepancy suggests that proactive IIs assist competitors in psychologically preparing for actual competition.

Interestingly, success was not associated with having retroactive IIs. Gotcher and Honeycutt (1989) speculated that the competitors in this scenario were focusing on the shortcoming of their actual performance. Yet through retroactivity competitors could bolster themselves for anticipated news of low ratings from a judge such that the delivery of the news is softened. Hence, retroactive IIs can play an educational role for the competitor to the extent that future performances may be adjusted. Not only can IIs better prepare competitors for the actual encounter through rehearsal, but they also may provide psychological support after the fact.

The result of Gotcher and Honeycutt's (1989) study has implications for coaches. For IIs to enhance positive outcomes, coaches need to encourage competitors to construct IIs with critics. Most of these IIs occurred with opponents, although the critic makes the decisions in the round. Yet the round is decided in the mind of the critic as opposed to the minds of the competitors (Thomas, 1981).

IIs with judges could be constructed from actual communication with judges as well as examining judges' ballots, judging philosophies, and discussions with other contestants concerning various judges. Actually talking with other contestants reflects "third-party uncertainty reduction" (Honeycutt, 1992). Sometimes there is the desire to reduce ambiguity about another's actions and behaviors before talking with the person. One way this is done is by asking for another person's opinion about the judge.

Coaches should encourage competitors to have proactive IIs in which they imagine successful outcomes. In addition, athletes should mentally rehearse the behavior reproduced in competition. Debaters could rehearse cross-examination questions and answers, refutations, first affirmative responses, case arguments, and exceptions. Individual event participants could focus attention on maintaining concentration in upcoming rounds. Gotcher and Honeycutt (1989) indicated that whatever problems the participants may have in competition could be minimized through positive IIs. In this regard, coaches could encourage retroactive IIs among their participants by having them play back the round in their minds and attempt to identify positive aspects of their performance while trying to reproduce those in future rounds.

Finally, IIs can be used to compensate for the lack of competitive experience. The more frequently that IIs were imagined about forensic competition, the more accurately they reflected reality and corresponded to success. Because a major portion of forensics is in the mind, it is prudent for coaches to encourage participants to imagine the rounds. If success and control in the actual rounds can be linked to concentration to the forensic task at hand, then IIs result in successful outcomes.

IIS AMONG BANKING EXECUTIVES

A powerful tool for managerial planning is IIs. Bryan, Berkos, Ross, and Croghan (2000) discussed the use of IIs among banking managers. They discussed how supervisors tell stories about their experiences with counseling employees. This experience, although relatively common, may be painful. It is rare for an employee not to require feedback regarding performance improvement at some point. The feedback may involve a variety of issues, including a lack of clear direction for the employee's work, a lack of the skills necessary to do the job, problems with self or family that impact an employee's performance, or even a miscommunication concerning expectations for performance (Stroul, 1992). These counseling sessions can address a number of problems identified in the employee's performance or run concurrently with performance reviews. Such feedback sessions appear to be conducted frequently in some companies and infrequently in others.

Burke (1996) reported that 79% of employees (out of 1,608 responses received) in a professional services firm he studied had been involved in employee counseling sessions. Unfortunately, the employees counseled believed the sessions were only moderately helpful in improving their performances, understanding of their strengths and weaknesses, and services to customers. Although the company provided management training, the managers in the organization felt that they had not been adequately trained to provide counseling and coaching.

Richmond, McCroskey, and Davis (1986) reported that counseling or feedback sessions are infrequent in organizations, although the employees report that the sessions may have positive outcomes. Supervisors often communicate using a top-down hierarchy and rarely alter their messages for a particular employee. A transactional approach to communication and the feedback process would be helpful, but unfortunately it is not within the quick-fix mentality that managers must often use in handling problematic situations.

The popular training and management press is filled with articles on coaching, counseling, and conducting performance appraisals. Some suggest steps in the coaching process, such as "(1) build mutual trust, (2) open the meeting, (3) get agreement on the performance problems, (4) explore solutions, (5) get a commitment from the employee to take action, and (6) handle excuses" (Phillips & Brown, 1993). Others suggest initiating small, informal discussions, not necessarily in the boss' office (Konrad, 1995). Some articles deal with the role confusion of managers and suggest that managers should clearly define their own roles within the organization prior to counseling an employee (Stroul, 1992). Others offer software programs that purportedly facilitate employee counseling and review sessions (McCune, 1997). Some articles emphasize the time element of feedback, cautioning that the employee should receive it as quickly as possible after the event has occurred (Bell & Zemke, 1992). Salters (1997) suggested that managers and supervisors skilled in employee counseling are less likely to have subsequent lawsuits filed by disgruntled employees. The general popularity of the employee counseling and feedback theme is reflected in an Internet search of employee counseling and coaching materials, which brought up over 500,000 hits (Infoseek, 1998).

There is no shortage of materials suggesting what to say when discussing an employee's performance. However, there is apparently little information recommending what should precede the feedback or counseling session. Supervisors need to get the most out of these sessions and achieve an understanding of needed behavioral change. This may be done through IIs.

The use of IIs can bring many benefits to the individual. As noted in chapter 3, these include increasing competence (through greater sensitivity, flexibility, and confidence), improving understanding (of self and others), and improving mood (by reducing primary and secondary tensions). Bryan et al. (2000) believed that these benefits could assist managers and supervisors in improving the efficacy of their counseling sessions with subordinates. Increased competence may provide the most benefit to a manger because the perception of the importance and veracity of the message conveyed to the direct report would certainly increase with increased perceptions of competence. Bryan et al. (2000) examined II characteristics of activity, retroactivity, and discrepancy in addition to the II functions of rehearsal and catharsis to assess II usage because these would most likely enhance the efficacy of counseling in the workplace and accrue the aforementioned benefits.

The participants included managers and supervisors of a medium-size full-service commercial bank with total assets of $1.4 billion located in Louisiana. Seventy-seven managers responded to a survey containing items from the SII (Honeycutt et al., 1992-1993). Based on responses to a job title question, three levels of managers/supervisors were identified: (a) supervisors, administrative assistants, specialists, banking officers (18%); (b) assistant vice presidents and sales and customer service managers (49%); and (c) vice presidents and/or branch managers (33%). The employees had an average of 9.2 years of actual management experience, ranging from less than 1 year to 31 years. Numerous managers (39%) reported receiving no additional management training subsequent to their formal education, whereas 33% reported participating in one or two sessions, and 29% reported receiving relatively extensive management training subsequent to their formal education.

The supervisors indicated they would be likely to have IIs with their employees. In addition, they had IIs about counseling sessions. Bryan et al. (2000) also found that the longer managers have been advising employees, the more likely they were to use IIs to aid in counseling situations. The data also revealed that managers used IIs for both rehearsal and catharsis. Although the managers were more likely to use IIs to rehearse for a counseling situation, they released emotions through having these IIs. Finally, the more likely the manager used IIs reflecting catharsis, the less discrepant the IIs were with the actual interaction. Therefore, if a manager imagined firing his or her employee for poor performance, his or her likelihood of actually firing the employee increased.

This research may be specific to the organizational culture within one corporation, and future researchers should examine multiple organizations to determine patterns of II usage across or within specific organization types. Additionally, Bryan et al. (2000) called for future research examining the relationship of management level to managers' IIs in relation to their employees as well as investigating the other uses of IIs within the organizational context beyond counseling situations.

IIS AND MUTUAL INFLUENCE

Roloff and Ifert (1998) discussed mutual influence in conversations and called for research on mutual influence in IIs. Mutual influence is a critical characteristic of all dialogue. Yet the action of one person is contingent on the action of the other and the inverse (McCall & Simmons, 1978). To show mutual influence, one must study the actions of at least two interactants and be able to observe behaviors enacted by two persons. Apparently IIs that reside within the mind are beyond the scope of mutual influence. Yet Roloff and Ifert (1998) believe that mutual influence can be extended to IIs because there are patterns that "suggest, but do not definitively demonstrate, the existence of mutual influence" (p. 115).

A problem with observing influence within a conversation is the restriction of observing actions and reactions without regard to time lag. Cappella (1985, 1987) indicated that mutual influence is only confirmed when the probability of an interactant's enactment of a particular behavior (e.g., interruptions), given his or her partner's prior actions, is different from what would be expected based on his or typical behavioral enactment. In other words, both communicators are affecting each other's behavior at levels beyond their baseline performances (Roloff & Ifert, 1998). Yet observing behaviors occurring only within a given conversation does not address whether the behaviors occurring during one conversation influence behavior enacted in subsequent conversations.

Yet there are definitive patterns in the imagined discourse. The person imagining the dialogue is more likely to initiate the interaction and speak more words (Honeycutt et al., 1990). As noted in chapter 2, individuals often replay prior conversations while planning for anticipated conversations. Hence, there is influence from prior conversations. Over half of IIs in one study served both rehearsal and review functions (Honeycutt et al., 1990). Recall how individuals reconstruct prior conversations and how the interaction might have been different if they had said other things. Individuals may be aware of the contingent nature of conversation and use that knowledge to devise alternative patterns.

Roloff and Ifert (1998) believe that IIs may themselves demonstrate mutual influence. Although IIs may be discrepant from actual talk, the rehearsal function affects actual communicative behavior. Jones and Gerard (1967) indicated how conversational behaviors reflect both mutual influences within the conversation and plans created prior to the conversation. They discussed four types of conversations: pseudocontingency, asymmetrical contingency, reactive contingency, and mutual contingency.

Pseudocontingency occurs when both interactants' behaviors emanate from their preinteraction plans. Pseudocontingency involves a conversation in which the speech is guided by a prior script. Mutual influence only regulates who has the speaking and listening roles at any given time in the conversation. This is highly ritualized, such as wedding vows and play scripts.

Asymmetrical contingency reflects conversations in which the statements of one interactant is preplanned while the statements of the other individual are in response to utterances made during the conversation. This can be related to proactive IIs and the rehearsal function of one interactant while the corresponding partner did not plan any statements in advance. Roloff and Ifert (1998) indicated how the initiator has the advantage of having imagined the upcoming encounter and can enact his or her plan while the target is "taken by surprise and can only react to what is said" (p. 120). This pattern implies that the II could affect the behaviors of both individuals by having a direct effect on the initiator and an indirect effect on the target that responds to the planned behaviors of the initiator.

Reactive contingency occurs when the behavior of both individuals is entirely affected by prior actions within the conversation. Yet a person exerts secondary influence over his or her own future behavior by directly affecting the partner's current behavior. No IIs are involved here.

Finally, mutual contingency is a pattern in which the behaviors of both individuals are determined partly by their preinteraction plans and partly by each other's current behavior. Hence, this type of contingency indicates that conversations can be both planned and spontaneous. This type of contingency involves both individuals having proactive IIs. A person may begin a conversation with a plan, but change or discard it during the interactions. This reflects the discrepancy characteristic of IIs.

Roloff and Ifert (1998) argued that IIs play a role in actual conversation, although these types of contingencies remain untested. There may be direct and indirect influence over a series of conversations.

IIS AND DECEPTION

Researchers have studied deception since 1920 (Marston, 1920). *Deception* can be defined as the intent to deceive someone by controlling information (e.g., transmitting verbal and nonverbal messages and/or manipulating situational cues) to alter another person's beliefs or understanding in a way that the deceiver knows is false (Buller & Burgoon, 1993). This definition is the most viable because it acknowledges that the transmission of false verbal information is not necessary for deception to occur. Communicators can create a false belief in someone's mind by communicating vague or ambiguous messages, concealing information from truthful messages, varying the intensity of truthful information through exaggeration and minimization, and manipulating environmental cues to create deceptive frames (Buller & Burgoon, 1993). This definition precludes intentionally transparent lies such as sarcasm and mistaken lies such as unknowingly providing false information.

Fontenot (1997) discussed the effects of IIs and information processing on the ability to detect deception. The social incentives to deceive are powerful (Bok, 1978). As Fontenot (1997) indicated, deception often harms the deceived, yet provides positive consequences for the deceiver. Buller and Burgoon (1993) reported how many people believe the ability to deceive others is an indispensable strategy for developing and maintaining satisfying social relationships and creating and maintaining a desired image. However, those who say they are behaving strategically when they lie, and say they are lying for the good of the other person, report that they do not want to be deceived (Fontenot, 1997).

The ability to deceive is a strategic communication skill. The ability to detect deception is an equally valuable skill. Researchers have investigated the degree to which age, self-monitoring ability, social skills, physical attractiveness, attention determinants, familiarity, ethnic background, general work experience, religious commitment, and gender affect one's ability to detect deception (Fontenot, 1997).

Many researchers have argued that deception detectors are not accurate. For example, Zuckerman and associates' (1985) findings are often cited, in which untrained observers were only accurate in detecting deception half of the time. Others have found different accuracy rates varying from a mean accuracy score of 63% for untrained observers to a mean accuracy rate of 77% for trained observers (Fontenot, 1997).

Recall from chapter 1 how IIs are a type of mindful activity. Langer (1989) distinguished between mindfulness, where people attend to their world and derive behavioral strategies based on current incoming information, and mindlessness, where new information is not being processed. Instead, prior scripts, written when similar information was once new, are stereotypically reenacted. Just as simple motor acts are often so overlearned that performance is automatic and mindless, social interactions are also mindless. According to Langer (1989), mindful communication requires actively using cognitive processes to overcome old, established ways of thinking to make distinctions and create new categories. These cognitive processes enable the individual to gain the following: an openness to new information, the awareness that more than one perspective exists, probabilistic or conditional thinking, and thinking in terms of process rather than the end result.

Mindfulness implies creative thought and attention to information. People are likely to be mindful when they encounter new situations for which they have no script (Langer, 1989). However, once situations are no longer new and the relevant schematic scripts are formed, people become mindless communicators. To the extent that people expect honest communication, there is little mindful processing of deception. In fact, some research has revealed that individuals are more accurate in labeling communication behaviors (e.g., filled pauses) as indicating deception when they are told that another person may be deceptive as opposed to not being told this information (Fontenot, 1997).

There is a truth bias in which communicators assume a source will provide both truthful information (McCornack & Parks, 1986). Even when forewarned about deceit, receivers still look for truth (Buller, Strzyzewski, & Comstock, 1991). To successfully identify deception, the observer must be mindful and pay close attention to the behavior of the deceiver and have a comparison model of the liar's honest behavior to compare with the current behavior (Knapp & Comadena, 1979).

There are several reasons that there is a relationship among IIs, deception, and deception detection. IIs involve a high degree of mindfulness, as does deception. Deceivers go through four distinct steps. First, they assess their motives: They examine the nature of the situation and their relationship with the target. Second, they appraise the alternative influence messages in their communication repertoire. Third, they select a particular message while forgoing others. Finally, they monitor the reactions of the target to formulate subsequent message choices (Buller & Burgoon, 1993). This process requires the deceiver to mindfully communicate during all of these steps.

Fontenot (1997) discussed how the rehearsal function of IIs assists in deception. She speculated that planned lies are harder to detect than spontaneous lies because planned lies allow for rehearsal. Four vocal cues are consistently related to deception: response length, speech errors, speech hesitations, and voice pitch. Compared with truthful messages, deceptive messages are characterized by shorter response lengths, higher pitch, more speech errors, and more speech hesitations (Buller & Burgoon, 1993). When people lie, they pause more and longer when answering a question. Recall chapter 3, in which Allen and Honeycutt (1997) investigated the impact of IIs on speech fluency and found people who engaged in IIs were more fluent. They had shorter speech onset latencies and shorter silent pause duration. In other words, IIs seem to control the speech errors present during deception. This finding suggests that rehearsing one's deception in terms of IIs might make messages more believable.

Recall from chapter 2 that *conversational sensitivity* refers to the ability to detect and decode the verbal and nonverbal cues in conversations (Daly et al., 1987). Conversational sensitivity consists of multiple dimensions and that two of these dimensions—conversational alternatives and detecting meanings—are positively associated with deception detection (Fontenot, 1997). Conversational alternatives refer to flexibility in communicating and being skilled at wording the same idea differently. Detecting meanings is the tendency to sense the purposes and hidden meanings in what others are saying. As noted in chapter 2, conversational alternatives are associated with variety and specificity. Detecting meanings is associated with retroactivity and specificity. Hence, having specific IIs may be related to the ability to detect deception. Clearly, future research needs to examine characteristics and functions of IIs in relation to deception detection.

IIS AND PRAYER

Is prayer a special type of II or completely different? According to the Gallup Survey on religion and practice in 1997, nine out of ten American adults say that they pray. Nearly all those who pray think their prayers are heard (97%) and are answered (95%). Gallup and Lindsay (1999) stated, "For most Americans, prayer is something that originates in the family, is centered in the home, grows in importance, and generates feelings of peace and hope" (p. 46). Gallup also reported that one of the outcomes of prayer is feeling more peaceful or hopeful. People believe prayer makes them better persons. This is related to the catharsis function of IIs. Furthermore, about one in four reports hearing a voice or seeing a vision as a result of prayer. They believe that a supreme being such as God, Jesus Christ, Jehovah, or the Lord hears them. Hence, this is not imagined interaction but real.

Internal Interactions Distinguished From Imagined Interactions

Williamson (1980) discussed prayer as a special case of intrapersonal communication. He defined *intrapersonal communication* as having a conversation with oneself. We learn how to intrapersonally communicate by modeling it on interpersonal communication in terms of actual conversations we have with others. Williamson (1980) wrote, "Only after learning how to converse intelligently with another person can an individual converse in a meaningful, adult way with himself" (p. 12).

　　Prayer can be understood as a type of intrapersonal communication that is influenced by interpersonal communication. Williamson discussed how prayer is not totally private or idiosyncratic. There are public prayers such as the Lord's Prayer, saying grace, and eulogies. Prayer is molded by various religious traditions and hence, like all intrapersonal communication, is a social product. Williamson provided examples of how prayer is different based on Benedictine spirituality, Franciscan spirituality, Catholicism, Evangelical, and Methodist spirituality. Thus, prayer as intrapersonal communication is an inner dialogue between the self and God, which is learned through the teachings offered by a variety of religious traditions.

　　Rosenblatt, Meyer, and Karis (1991-1992) distinguished between internal and imagined interactions after interviewing a sample of 10 seminarians and 8 spiritual directors about their communication with God and a comparison sample of five psychologists who had been in therapy and talked about their interactions with their therapists. The interviewees ranged in age from 24 to 63 (average of 44). The spiritual directors in the study had formal education in spiritual direction and were Roman Catholics. Their goal is to help others come to terms with God, differentiate from a formal religion they view as spiritually stifling, and find their own spiritual meanings. The 10 seminarians were Lutheran.

The third sample was designed to give a comparison base of interactions with other people. It consisted of 22 psychologists randomly selected from the membership of a state psychological association and a local association of Jungian analysts. Five of the 22 had been in therapy. This sample was used because of similarities in the areas of life and minds that religion and psychotherapy address. Rosenblatt et al. (1991-1992) discussed how there is a focus on the search for personal, emotional, or spiritual truth—a struggle to connect with other people in one's past, and an attempt to discover order in the past, present, and future.

Interactions with God were experienced as real, not imagined, and God was viewed as all knowing. For example, the psychologists reported that the therapist in their internal interactions was imagined. All seminarians and spiritual directors said that God was real in the internal interaction. They said that, during the internal interaction, God might reply through words said by others, words that came to the mind of the respondent, and feelings of peace. Four reported direct verbal messages from God including, "Speak to my heart" or "I want you to get married; I have something to give you" (Rosenblatt et al., 1991-1992, p. 90).

Prayer was distinguished from these internal interactions. Half of the seminarians and spiritual directors felt that their internal interactions with God were like their prayers, whereas seven others felt that their interactions with God were more spontaneous. Prayer may be one sided, in which the individual praying sets the agenda. Internal interactions with God were reported as being more two-sided and spontaneous rather than preplanned. In distinguishing internal interaction from imagined interactions, Rosenblatt and his associates (1991-1992) stated, "Because the seminarians and spiritual directors experienced interaction with God as real, it seems appropriate to call the images of interaction studied in this research "internal interaction" (pp. 89-90).

All of the seminarians and spiritual directors reported that their internal interactions with God helped them connect with their true self and to be more honest with themselves. Yet they could not clearly separate themselves from God. God and the self were fused. Hence, it can be argued that they were talking with a part of themselves. This is analogous to self-talk or monologue, talking with an inner, spiritual self. Kubler-Ross distinguished the social, intellectual, physical, and spiritual selves. Hence, the social self in an internal interaction could be communicating with a spiritual self. Rosenblatt and his associates (1991-1992) discussed the problem of separating aspects of multiple selves and wondered about the boundaries between self and other when a significant other in internal interactions is God that is seen as part of oneself. What is the proper way to characterize the self?

All three groups reported that solving problems was an outcome of their internal interactions. Yet their reports actually seemed to reflect the catharsis function discussed in chapter 3. Rosenblatt and his colleagues (1991-1992) provided the example of a psychologist indicating how the interactions helped him let go of issues while a seminarian reported how the internal interactions with God allowed him to feel calm and discuss feelings. Another seminarian reported, "I can lay on the table what society won't let me lay out" (Rosenblatt et al., 1991-1992, p. 93). This is similar to the boldness function discussed in chapter 7 to the extent that individuals can say things internally without fear of retribution. For psychologists, the nurturance reflected the supportiveness of the imagined therapist.

The compensation function of IIs was apparent in some internal interactions. Recall from chapter 3 that IIs may be used to compensate for the lack of real interaction. Many spiritual directors and seminarians discussed how they were in social encounters where full honesty about their religious beliefs was risky, where people were uninterested in the thoughts of others, or where their opinions were unwelcome. Hence, internal interaction with God was satisfying and used to compensate for discussing their feelings with the hostile others.

Feelings of support and nurturance were also mentioned. Their internal interactions with God or the therapist helped sustain them in difficult times. For psychologists, they felt nurtured through imagining the support of the therapist. For seminarians and spiritual directors, nurturance was experienced in terms of a loving, idealized, perfect God.

The interviews provided support for distinguishing IIs from internal interactions. Rosenblatt et al. (1991-1992) called for future research to explore how people decide that internal interaction with God is real. Some of the seminarians indicated that sometimes, in their internal interactions, if they were not sure whether God was there or not and did not have a strong sense of God's presence later, there was more direct dialogue with God. It would be interesting to explore the sense of reality to internal interactions with God. Further, from the perspective of different religious faiths, how does interaction with God differ? The experience of God by Catholics and Protestants might differ from the experience of God by Hindus, Muslims, or other faiths. For example, Balinese Hindus may experience possession by spiritual entities that range widely on a dimension of good versus evil (Rosenblatt et al., 1991-1992).

To conclude this section, IIs occur with significant others in the form of human beings. Talking with God reflects prayer and what Rosenblatt et al. (1991-1992) called *internal interactions*. Some of the functions of IIs and internal interactions are similar including compensation, catharsis, and self-understanding. Yet rehearsal only occurs in IIs because the interaction with God in prayer is perceived as real. Yet there must be more research on clearly differentiating aspects of the self because it can be argued that talking with God, which is seen as part of oneself, reflects self-talk or internal monologues.

SUMMARY

There are limitless opportunities to examine the functions of IIs in an assortment of contexts. IIs have shown that they help cancer patients in communicating with doctors and family members. Emotions are released through the catharsis function. Furthermore, as noted, some individuals release tension and stress through recalling old conversations with deceased individuals. By definition, IIs occur with real-life significant others. Yet a retroactive II with a deceased person occurs. However, it is impossible to have proactive IIs with a deceased person.

IIs have been examined among homeless mothers. Their IIs reflect learning from the past and hoping for a better future. They have IIs with ex-partners while wishing the relationship was not over. Yet some of their IIs deal with abuse and chemical dependency. A number of IIs were with newly created social families in terms of having IIs with roommates at the homeless shelter.

The rehearsal function of IIs has been examined in forensic competition. Similar to instilling mental imagery in athletic competition, IIs help debaters prepare questions and responses before their debates. IIs in organizations were reviewed with rehearsal and catharsis emerging as important functions for banking managers. In addition, the managers used IIs proactively before counseling subordinates.

IIs and forms of mutual influence were examined in which individuals may imagine how they can influence the responses of others before encountering them. Pseudocontingency occurs when both interactants' behaviors emerge from preinteraction plans. IIs help constitute many preinteraction plans.

The rehearsal function of IIs may assist individuals for the purposes of deception. Planned lies are harder to detect than spontaneous lies. Yet having specific IIs may also be related to the ability to detect deception. IIs were distinguished from prayer. While praying, individuals believe they are actually communicating with a deity. Hence, it is not imagined, but real from their perspective.

Chapter 8

IIs and Enhancing

Effective Communication

A s noted in chapter 3, there are therapeutic benefits to having IIs, such as catharsis, self-understanding, and rehearsal. We experience a variety of emotions when imagining conversations. IIs associated with positive emotions occur less frequently and with less retroactivity than those with mixed emotions (Zagacki et al., 1992). This finding is somewhat surprising insofar as we might expect individuals to dwell upon pleasant communicative episodes to extend the positive feelings. One possibility is that pleasant communicative experiences, once acknowledged, are simply taken for granted and not recalled frequently in the form of an II. Another possibility is that an individual's desire for internal (emotional) consistency leads them to circumvent review of pleasant communicative episodes in the form of IIs. To do so might create the possibility that one would discover potentially discrepant and therefore unpleasant information. Hence, it would be wise to train individuals to imagine positive scenarios to alleviate anxiety or even depression. This chapter details suggestions for improving IIs to achieve more productive outcomes intrapersonally and in actual encounters. In addition, tips about how to have better IIs after real encounters have already occurred are discussed to better understand what transpired.

POSITIVE FEELINGS AND DEPRESSION USING IMAGERY

IIs make us feel happy or sad as well as having mixed feelings. In some cases, they result in depression. For example, Schultz (1978) investigated the use of imagery to alleviate depression. He studied four imagery conditions across 60 depressed male psychiatric patients. One condition labeled the *aggressive imagery procedure* had depressed males recalling someone saying something that angered the self. In the socially gratifying imagery condition, the individual was instructed to recall someone saying something that was very pleasing. The *positive imagery* condition had the patient recall a place he used to visit to relax. Finally, the *free imagery* condition had the patient reporting all images, thoughts, fantasies, and ideas that occurred to him without trying to direct his thoughts.

Ratings of depressive feelings taken 10 minutes after the imagery induction revealed that the first two conditions produced lower levels of depression than the less socially oriented conditions. The aggressive and socially gratifying inductions resulted in the patient having retroactive IIs that were negative and pleasant, respectively. Schultz (1978) also reported that in comparing the socially gratifying and positive imagery conditions, depression was lowered after the socially gratifying induction.

There is a therapeutic goal to train individuals to have IIs that make them feel better. Recall the findings on the dysfunctional use of IIs for the lonely. Lonely individuals reported fewer IIs (Edwards et al., 1988). Yet when they had them, they were discrepant from what actually happened in their actual conversations. Klinger (1990) reported that daydreaming may make us feel more relaxed, stimulate us, organize our lives, help us be more effective in social situations through exploration and rehearsal, provide a medium for growth, foster finding creative solutions to problems, create empathy, and move us toward making decisions.

Klinger (1990) noted the benefit of rehearsal. He wrote:

> When psychologists talk about daydreaming being a kind of spontaneous rehearsal for real life, that is not just a metaphor. Our daydream images represent parts of the same brain mechanisms at work that generate our actions. (p. 291)

When we rehearse messages and use the same brain mechanisms that generate action, the benefits of the rehearsal influence our physical behavior.

THERAPEUTIC BENEFITS OF DAYDREAMING

Klinger (1990) reported numerous therapeutic benefits of daydreaming. They may provide relaxation, stimulation, help organize our lives, and improve physical skills through mental practice. Additionally, daydreaming may help us in social encounters by rehearsing conversations. Other benefits include providing opportunities for growth and self-therapy, helping us make decisions, facilitating creativity in terms of solving problems, instilling perspective taking or empathy, and helping to foster more desirable personality traits.

Controlled daydreaming is used to relax us in many contexts. We can use daydreams when feeling harried by imagining pleasant events so that our emotions are gradually calmed. Daydreaming can also have a calming effect by letting us work through problems until we have a sense of how to handle them.

Daydreaming can enhance decision making. We often become paralyzed by information overload when having to make critical decisions such that we are unable to decide among numerous options. Daydreaming about contingencies facilitates plans of action. Klinger (1990) reported an unpublished study among a group of women who were asked to think about a difficult personal decision and indicate how committed they were to a course of action. The decisions involved deciding whether to terminate a relationship with their boyfriends, whether to change college majors, and where to travel on an ensuing vacation. A control group performed some math problems and went home while two other groups spent time in controlled daydreaming and imagined interactions.

One group imagined in greater detail the positive benefits of one course of action they had thought about such as leaving their boyfriends. The second daydreaming group imagined in detail various things they would do to carry out the course of action. This involved having an imagined interaction in which they told the boyfriend about their decision, moving out of the shared apartment, dividing property, and spending a week with an old friend to feel emotional release from the termination of the relationship. Before they left the daydreaming session, these women indicated again how committed they felt about their decision they had just imagined.

Three weeks later, they received a survey that asked again about where they stood on their decision. The women who had the imagined interaction had moved the furthest toward making a firm decision. The group who did the math problems was the furthest from a decision than they had been 3 weeks before. The group that only imagined nice benefits from the course of action were more committed to the decision right after the daydreaming session, but over the 3-week time period regressed back to their original indecision. The findings suggest that if you wish to make a decision, you benefit from imagined interactions so that you become aware of potential problems, which also makes you feel more comfortable about deciding.

Aside from enhancing decision making, daydreaming is also beneficial in terms of self-stimulation. Individuals in boring jobs often daydream to escape from the monotony and tedium of their work. Swimming pool lifeguards, truck drivers, tractor drivers, security guards, and sales clerks on slow days deliberately daydream, although two thirds of these individuals acknowledge that daydreaming makes them less alert during the job (Klinger, 1990).

Gold, Gold, Milner, and Robertson (1986-1987) found that the daydreams of those who were mentally healthy felt better after daydreaming, whereas the less mentally healthy felt worse. Yet even unhappy daydreams can help us work through grief and sorrow. Cartwright (1984) studied the night dreams of women going through divorce. Women who dreamed about their marital status reported less depression than women going through divorce who did not dream.

Daydreaming is also positively related to empathy and perspective taking. A study in Minnesota had individuals beeped while listening to a recording of others telling stories about emotional episodes in their lives. The individuals reported more empathy for the storytellers and reported emotions similar to the storytellers when they were visualizing the storyteller's experiences vividly. Klinger (1990) reported other studies in which high school students who were listening to recordings of people describing their emotional experiences reported more empathy when daydreaming. When imagining interaction with others, we gain a better sense of what it must be like to experience what happened to the others, which facilitates our understanding of them.

We need additional research on the therapeutic uses of daydreaming in the form of IIs. Further evidence of the general and therapeutic functions of IIs is presented next in the form of journal accounts that some of my students collected. Having been exposed to the II concept, students often report having them, although they had not previously thought about the experience as an instance of imagined interaction. Journal accounts of IIs tend to be more impressionistic and reveal more about emotions and self-understanding than survey data.

Box 8.1 is an account of an II discussed by Honeycutt (1989), where rehearsal helped in enhancing confidence, although the actual conversation did not fulfill expectations because the individual rehearsed the wrong script. However, she believed that the act of rehearsing was helpful.

BOX 8.1

II Used for Rehearsal

A couple of weeks ago, you gave to us a survey to do on imagined interactions. After doing the survey, I realized that I never really thought about all of the imagined interactions that I actually have. I guess I just never really paid much attention before our discussions about them in class. Recently, I had to confront my father about moving out of the dorm and into an apartment. I was quite nervous about the whole confrontation, so before I discussed the issue with him, I kind of rehearsed what I was going to say to him and I tried to anticipate his reaction.

Our spring break is when I had to talk to my father, so for about 2 weeks beforehand, I was rehearsing. It seemed like every time I would think about it,

I would change my approach a little bit. But, my father's reaction, in my mind, was always the same. He would tell me that he did not want me to move into an apartment. In my imagination, I would tell him of all the benefits an apartment would have. I would have more privacy, there would not be as much noise so it would be easier to study, it is less expensive than the dorm and a meal plan and on and on.

The time finally arose when I had to confront him. Again, I imagined what I was going to say to him and then I went ahead and opened the discussion. To my surprise, I did not even use my plan of action. I did not even list the benefits of the apartment vs. the dorm. Nevertheless, we discussed it and my father agreed to my moving out which also contradicted my imagined interaction. I thought that this was kind of strange because usually my imagined interactions were similar in at least some ways to the actual conversation, but this one was completely opposite. At first I thought that all of that "practicing" was just a waste of time, since I did not use what I had practiced, but I think I was a little more confident about the discussion since I had gone over in my head the points of view that I wanted to get across. Maybe this helped since he agreed to let me move out. In this case, I am glad that they were different from the outcome. If they had gone the way I imagined, I would still be living in the dorm next semester.

PLANNING AND IIS

The rehearsal function of IIs is predicated on the assumption that planning for certain conversations is helpful in achieving goals. Allen and Edwards (1991) found that participants who engaged in rehearsal prior to discussing a friend's drinking problem and suggesting that the friend seek help used a greater number and variety of compliance-gaining messages than participants who engaged in a task aimed at distracting them from planning. They also found that participants who reported a high tendency to rehearse mentally, regardless of whether they were in the distractor task or the planning task, used more message strategies during the actual conversation compared with individuals who reported a low tendency to rehearse mentally.

PLANNING AND CREATIVITY

Planning contingencies via IIs is a creative process. One way to plan contingencies is through brainstorming, in which individuals generate ideas without fear of criticism (Gordon, 1961; Osborn, 1953). Another technique is the generate and judge model. Anderson (1985) argued that productive, creative thinking involves the generation of ideas and the judgment of quality of the ideas. Support has been found for judging the quality of ideas when generating them.

Johnson, Parrott, and Stratton (1968) compared a brainstorming group and a comparison group using the generate and judge model. The brainstorming group was instructed to generate one optimal solution to a problem. The other group was told to generate as many solutions as possible. The quality of the solutions from the brainstorming group was lower than that of the solution group that was trained to generate and judge solutions.

Planning for communication is a creative process. When having proactive IIs, individuals are engaging in generating and judging ideas as they think of contingency plans. Allen (1993) examined proactive IIs and contingency planning among 105 students. She asked the participants if they developed different contingency plans while preparing for anticipated encounters and how discrepant their IIs were from actual encounters. She found that the participants used IIs to generate contingencies for the self and for the other interaction partner. They envisioned a number of different ways that the other person could respond to what the self says during the II. Recall from chapter 2 that the self dominates most of the conversation during IIs. Yet when thinking of contingencies, taking the perspective of the other improves plan generation. Furthermore, discrepancy was negatively associated with generating contingencies for the partner. In other words, generating other contingencies resulted in the IIs matching what happened during actual conversations. Hence, individuals should be encouraged to plan strategic interactions beforehand rather than waiting to see what occurs during the encounters.

PRACTICING CONVERSATIONS THROUGH IIS

There are numerous instances of using mental imagery to enhance athletic performance. Indeed, some athletes, including basketball legend Michael Jordan, imagine optimal capacity performances before competition. They also report mentally replaying plays to facilitate future performances. Field goal kickers often imagine the football crossing the goal posts before they kick the ball. This positive imagery reshapes and reflects the old adage practice makes perfect.

Individuals who imagine conversations are more competent in a variety of communicative encounters. Conversational sensitivity, in which individuals read between the lines of what others are saying, is one indicator of communication competence. Sensitive people listen for feelings besides the literal content of what is said. Indeed, this may be why women, who tend to spend more time imagining conversations, are better at keeping real conversations flowing. Individuals gain more self-understanding, clarifying their feelings about people and topics, by thinking about interactions. For example, as Nicholas keeps imagining an upcoming conversation with Claire, he realizes devoting attention to it must mean he likes her. This is also referred to as *intrusive thinking*. According to Fisher (1994), individuals who are infatuated with someone and falling in love report spending from 85% to 100% of their time thinking about their partners. Many emotions are felt at this stage, including elation, hope, apprehension, uncertainty, shyness, fear of rejection, helplessness, irrationality, uncontrollability, and longing for reciprocity. Recall the compensation function of IIs in which individuals imagine talking with their partner outside of his or her physical presence. IIs are a part of intrusive thinking and maintaining the relationship as noted in chapter 4.

Indeed, IIs help keep relationships alive despite physical separations. "Out of sight, but in mind" reminds lovers of the others' delightful qualities. For example, one of my students wrote:

> Because my present girlfriend is living in New Orleans this semester, I often have imagined interactions about the two of us. For instance, I often imagine us embracing and kissing when we see each other on Fridays. These imagined interactions are often fulfilled and then some.

As noted in chapter 3, IIs can improve mood by reducing tensions. For example, one of my students fantasized an II with an ex-lover who terminated their relationship. He apologized for the hurt he caused and said how wrong he was to let her go. She responded that she hated him and that she was better off with her present boyfriend. This II, occurring in the post-termination stage of relationship decay, helped her achieve closure and move on with greater self-esteem. Box 8.2 presents the sample journal account of this and indicates how open communication would have helped.

BOX 8. 2

IIs With an Ex-Relational Partner

I had a relationship in high school with a girl that was serious as far as high school relationships go. We dated for almost a year and then broke up. Even though I was the one who terminated the relationship I was also the one who was the loneliest afterwards. I can remember keeping up with the girl through our mutual friends. I wanted to know who she was dating, what they were doing, and whether she still liked me. I would have imagined interactions with this girl in which I would tell her the things that bothered me about her. She would change the behaviors that I did not like and then we would get back together.

For whatever reasons, I was not able to come straight out and talk to her about the problems I was having with her. Instead, I just terminated the relationship. I often imagined being with this girl years afterward and would go over in my mind things we had said and what could have been said different—sort of a cross between fantasizing and imagined interaction. A couple of years after high school and probably 4 years after we had dated, we met in a college town and had a few dates. Within a very short time, maybe 2 weeks, our relationship was right back to where it was before I terminated it with her in high school. Again she showed behavior that was close to that which I had not been able to accept in high school and again I terminated the relationship. This time we both sort of broke contact and did not make an effort to reach one another. Although I still think about this person on occasion, it is only because she was a big part of my past and I tend to reflect on my past experiences and relationships at times.

The man who wrote this journal entry was having retroactive IIs. Conversely, proactive IIs help individuals plan strategies, reduce primary tension (occurring before or at the beginning of interactions), and seek input from others. Planning strategies increases successes and reduces embarrassments. For example, before asking for a date we usually rehearse what to say, and what to say if he or she says no. Practicing IIs boosts confidence by reducing evaluation apprehension even when actual encounters differ from those practiced. One woman, who practiced informing her father about moving off campus, wrote "I thought that all of that 'practicing' was just a waste of time, since I did not use what I had practiced, but I think I was a little more confident about the discussion since I had gone over in my head the points of view that I wanted to get across." IIs with admired or trusted people—assuming we realize the conversations are imaginary—are excellent ways to consider other points of view before acting.

Retroactive IIs help individuals understand what took place, review strategies, and reduce secondary tension (occurring as a result of the interaction). For example, Sara thinks over her speech's unexpectedly warm reception and realizes classmates judged her, as she judged them, on behavior, not subjective angst. She replays what she said and how she said it, and she decides to present her next assignment the same way, except for adding a final summary to clarify her main idea. Even if Sara's speech were bad, replaying it several times would help. It would release her pent-up feelings and emotions through the II function of catharsis in which she could reduce the interaction's negative impact and lessen the next speech's trauma. Indeed, behaviorists use a similar approach called *implosion therapy*. Patients imagine phobias as graphically and specifically as possible and usually find negative effects collapse from repeated exposure.

How Should We Practice IIs?

Practicing an II is easy and may be quite enjoyable depending on the topic. You imagine talking with an individual and contemplate what he or she might say. The scene of the imagined encounter could be anywhere, such as a room at your home, in an office building, or on the phone. Practicing a variety of specific IIs retroactively leads to enhanced sensitivity and results in greater ease and confidence when talking (Honeycutt, Zagacki, & Edwards, 1992-1993). Following is a brief discussion of each II characteristic and how to enhance that characteristic for more effective conversations.

FREQUENCY

Activity or the frequency of having IIs is associated with being able to use irony or sarcasm in conversations, catching hidden meanings in puns, and being able to effectively paraphrase what another person said in a conversation (Honeycutt et al., 1992-1993). It is also associated with sensing who likes whom in social conversations. As noted in chapter 2, loneliness is associated with the lack of IIs. Thinking of IIs may help prepare for conversational encounters. It also can enhance perspective taking and empathy.

RETROACTIVITY

Tips for retroactive IIs include returning to the situation and mentally re-creating the context of the encounter. In fact, you may want to take refresher notes soon after the event. Try to identify what you did well. Identify key factors in the interaction. Think of alternative actions you might have taken to improve consequences. Try to enhance empathy by role-playing the encounter from the other's point of view.

PROACTIVITY

Research reveals that proactivity is associated with sensing how well people really like each other in social encounters (Honeycutt et al., 1992-1993). Tips for proactive IIs involve relaxing ahead of the anticipated encounter. Be specific in imagining the scene of the encounter and what you and the other interactors say. Attempt to imagine the encounter from start to finish. Think about using role-playing rehearsals when possible.

SPECIFICITY

Recall from chapter 2 that specificity involves verbal and visual imagery in which lines of dialogue are envisioned as well as the scene of the II. Specificity is related to conversational sensitivity. Specificity is associated with detecting meanings in conversations (Honeycutt et al., 1992-1993) including noticing double meanings, finding hidden meanings in what others are saying, forecasting where a conversation is headed, and predicting what another person is going to say before he or she even says it. Specificity is also related to the ability to think of tactful ways of communicating. It is clear that thinking about specific statements to say and what others will say has conversational benefits. An important tip is to keep your mind focused on your messages and anticipate what another might say. In this regard, Honeycutt (1998-1999) found that individuals in secure, romantic relationships rehearse dialogue and have low discrepancy to the extent that what is imagined comes to pass in real encounters. IIs that are detailed in verbal and visual imagery, such as envisioning the scene of the encounter, are associated with higher quality romances.

VALENCE

The power of positive thinking was made famous in the 20th century by Norman Vincent Peale. He believed in the power of optimism. Indeed, a major component of happiness across the life span is optimism in terms of refusing to accept setbacks or hindrances (Myers & Diener, 1995). Recall from chapter 2 that IIs vary in terms of how pleasant they are. Individuals may have positive, negative, and mixed emotions depending on the topic and the interaction partner. A guideline for more effective IIs is to think positively.

VARIETY

We have IIs with different people as well as on a number of topics (see chap. 2). Variety is related to flexibility in communication as individuals think of a number of alternative ways to state their views. Competent communicators are able to word the same thought in different ways. Variety is related to being tactful in terms of knowing when to say the right thing at the right time (Honeycutt et al., 1992-1993).

Having a variety of IIs over a particular topic can provide a mechanism in which contingency plans are envisioned to prepare for the possible responses of others. An example of this is in the following journal account by a student who wrote about experimenting with different types of messages in his IIs and how helpful this was. He wrote:

> Imagined interactions provide an opportunity for individuals in a relationship to "experiment" with approaches they would not usually consider part of their inherent personality. Sometimes, I'm not very open with my partner. I withdraw and don't express myself. By using an II, I can imagine what would have occurred had I expressed my feelings and opinions more.

Contingency planning is taught in forensic competition to debaters. Effective debaters anticipate the rebuttals of those with opposing viewpoints. Ideally, the opposing views are refuted through persuasive arguments and claims.

Of course, it is possible to dwell too much on the opposing viewpoints of others. When this occurs, the individual may lose sight of his or her own positions and become defensive rather than collaborative. Indeed, as noted in the following sections, there are some things to avoid when having IIs to produce more effective communication.

DISCREPANCY

Avoid having discrepant IIs. Discrepancy is associated with loneliness and dysfunctional communication. As noted in chapter 2, discrepancy is negatively associated with communication competence. Discrepancy has been related to catastrophizing (Honeycutt & Cantrill, 2001). Catastrophizing occurs when what is imagined is quite negatively discrepant from what is likely to or actually did occur. For example, you might imagine requesting a loan from your closest friend. She or he snarls, "No, you should live on a budget," and stomps out. Yet, in real life, she or he simply hands over the money. Catastrophizing often results from poor self-concept or overgeneralizing. That is, "No one likes me" and "Stanford hasn't accepted me; no school will accept me." Such catastrophic expectations/assessments ultimately become self-fulfilling prophecies when real-life interactions are avoided.

The following journal account highlights how discrepancy is associated with loneliness and the positive benefits of imagining conversations. The student kept the journal after being exposed to IIs:

> Loneliness is something I used to suffer from until the last two or three years. There are certain predictors of loneliness that accurately depict the way I used to be; having few, yet discrepant imagined interactions. The fact of the matter is, I don't recall having any imagined interactions when I was younger. Although I can't recall many instances from my own life, I imagine how frustrating it must be if you can never predict how a conversation will go. Non-lonely people have a variety of imagined interactions, whereas lonely

people have very few imagined interactions. Now, I often have imagined interactions after an argument with the person in a calm and collected manner, expressing how I feel about the situation. This makes me feel better and builds confidence for future encounters.

MANAGING CONFLICT

As noted in chapter 5, keeping conflict alive occurs when individuals revisit old conflicts and plot or justify revenge. For example, the process of re-experiencing romantic arguments can act as negative preinteraction stimuli for a subsequent encounter. "He made me mad; I'll walk out if he does it again." Thus, conflicts are extended and rekindled. However, conflicts can be terminated and resolved.

IIs can be used to reduce conflict. Bury the hurt and think about compromise and tension reduction instead. I am not saying to "forgive and forget." Yet research has revealed that forgiveness is associated with being empathetic or taking the perspective of another, as opposed to avoiding personal and psychological contact with the offender. Alternatively, some individuals seek revenge based on feelings of righteous indignation, in which one desires harm to come to the offender (McCullough et al., 1998).

Avoid Rumination

Recall from chapter 5 that rumination is where individuals repetitively focus on themselves in terms of negative thoughts. Ruminators may overanalyze the causes of negative events as well as imagining bad outcomes. Rumination is related to depression (Lyubomirsky et al., 1999). Think of positive scenarios. Negative thinking results in reduced motivation as well as imagining failed problem-solving efforts even if the pessimistic thoughts never come to fruition (Teasdale, 1983).

SELF-DOMINANCE

Egocentrism occurs when we give ourselves a much more central role in IIs than what is likely to, or actually did, occur. This tendency includes overestimating our control over events (the illusion of control bias), overestimating our contributions to jointly produced products (the self-centered bias), and claiming undo credit for successes (the self-serving bias; Fincham & Bradley, 1989). For example, it is rare and almost unnatural to imagine listening to long monologues or lectures by others. We tend to see ourselves talking and our partner listening. Yet in reality, conversations are usually more evenly divided. Concentrating too much on what we want to say in imaginary encounters leaves us unprepared when partners say more than anticipated and lacking responses to probes, praise, questions, or compliments. Only by recognizing our tendency for egocentrism and concentrating on the words of others can we enhance active listening and increase conversational sensitivity.

SUMMARY

IIs are a natural and common phenomena we can use to improve our lives. Visualizing conversations before or after they take place has several major benefits. We become more competent conversationalists, improve our understanding of self and others, keep important relationships alive, and reduce our tensions. IIs are easy to practice and easy to do. An old maxim is, "I stuck my foot in my mouth." This maxim is less likely to occur if individuals have proactive IIs, avoid discrepancy, do not ruminate over conflict, and are self-dominant in the II. The act of imagining conversation tends to be helpful even if there is discrepancy because alternative messages may be used more effectively. IIs allow for a greater flexibility in communicating messages.

REFERENCES

Abelson, R. P. (1976). Script processing in attitude formation and decision-making. In J. S. Carroll & J. W. Payne (Eds.), *Cognition and social behavior* (pps. 33-46). Hillsdale, NJ: Erlbaum.

Ainsworth, M. D. S., Blehar, M. C., Waters, E., & Wall, S. (1978). *Patterns of attachment: A psychological study of the strange situation.* Hillsdale, NJ: Erlbaum.

Allen, T. H. (1990). The effects of Machiavellianism on imagined interaction. *Communication Research Reports, 7,* 116-120.

Allen T. H. (1993, April). *Planning and creativity: Is more better?* Paper presented at the annual Southern States Communication Association Conference, Miami, FL.

Allen, T. H. (1994, November). *Absence makes the mind work harder: Imagined interactions and coping with geographical separation.* Paper presented at the Speech Communication Association Conference, New Orleans, LA.

Allen, T. H., & Berkos, K. M. (1998, November). *A functional approach to imagined interaction: Examining conflict-linkage and aggression.* Paper presented at the National Communication Association Conference, New York.

Allen, T. H., & Edwards, R. (1991, November). *The effects of planning and imagined interaction on message strategy use.* Paper presented at the annual National Communication Association Conference, Atlanta, GA.

Allen, T. H., & Honeycutt, J. M. (1997). Planning, imagined interaction, and the nonverbal display of anxiety. *Communication Research, 24,* 64-82.

American Cancer Society. (1990). *Cancer facts and figures—1990.* New York: Author.

Anderson, J. R. (1980). *Cognitive psychology and its implications.* San Francisco: W. H. Freeman.

Anderson, J. R. (1983). *The architecture of cognition.* Cambridge, MA: Harvard University Press.

Anderson, J. R. (1985). *Cognitive psychology.* New York: W. H. Freeman.

Bales, R. F. (1970). *Personality and interpersonal behavior.* New York: Holt, Rinehart, & Winston.

Bartholomew, K. (1990). Avoidance of intimacy: An attachment perspective. *Journal of Social and Personal Relationships, 7,* 147-178.

Bartholomew, K. (1993). From childhood to adult relationships: Attachment theory and research. In S. Duck (Ed.), *Understanding relationship processes: Vol. 2. Learning about relationships* (pp. 30-62). Thousand Oaks, CA: Sage.

Beatty, M. J., & McCrosky, J. C. (1997). It's in our nature: Verbal aggressiveness as temperamental expression. *Communication Quarterly, 45,* 446-460.

Beatty, M. J., McCrosky, J. C., & Heisel, A. D. (1998). Communication apprehension as temperamental expression: A communibiological paradigm. *Communication Monographs, 65,* 197-219.

Bell, C., & Zemke, R. (1992). On-target feedback. *Training, 29,* 36-42.

Bell, R. A., & Daly, J. A. (1984). The affinity-seeking function of communication. *Communication Monographs, 51,* 91-115.

Berg, J. H., & Piner, K. E. (1989). Social relationships and the lack of social relationships. In S. Duck with R. Cohen Silver (Ed.), *Personal relationships and social support* (pp. 140-158). Newbury Park, CA: Sage.

Berger, C. R. (1988). Planning, affect and social action generation. In L. Donohew, H. E. Sypher, & E. T. Higgins (Eds.), *Communication, social cognition and affect* (pp. 93-116). Hillsdale, NJ: Erlbaum.

Berger, C. R. (1993). Goals, plans, and mutual understanding in relationships. In S. Duck (Ed.), *Individuals in relationships* (pp. 30-59). Newbury Park, CA: Sage.

Berger, C. R. (1997). *Planning strategic interaction: Attaining goals through communicative action.* Mahwah, NJ: Erlbaum.

Berger, C. R., & Bell, R. A. (1988). Plans and the initiation of social relationships. *Human Communication Research, 15,* 217-235.

Berkos, K.M. (1999). *Students' imagined interactions in reaction to teacher misbehaviors.* Unpublished master's thesis, California State University, Long Beach.

Berkos, K. M., Allen, T. H., Kearney, P., & Plax, T. G. (2001). When norms are violated: Imagined interactions as processing and coping mechanisms. *Communication Monographs, 68,* 289-300.

Berry, J. W. (1984). Cultural relations in plural societies: Alternatives to segregation and their sociopsychological implications. In N. Miller & M. Brewer (Eds.), *Groups in contact* (pp. 177-207). New York: Academic Press.

Berry, J. W., Kim, U., & Boski, P. (1987). Psychological acculturation of immigrants. In Y. Y. Kim & W. B. Gudykunst (Eds.), *Cross-cultural adaptation: Current approaches*. Beverly Hills, CA: Sage.

Blalock, H. M. (1969). *Theory construction: From verbal to mathematical formulations*. Englewood Cliffs, NJ: Prentice-Hall.

Bok, S. (1978). *Lying: Moral choices in public and private life*. New York: Pantheon.

Boon, S. D., & Sulsky, L. M. (1997). Attributions of blame and forgiveness in romantic relationships: A policy-capturing study. *Journal of Social Behavior and Personality, 12*, 19-44.

Bormann, E. G.(1985). Symbolic convergence theory: A communication formulation. *Journal of Communication, 35*, 128-136.

Bowlby, J. (1979). *The making and breaking of affectional bonds*. London: Tavistock.

Braiker, H. B., & Kelley, H. H. (1979). Conflict development of close relationships. In R. L. Burgess & T. L. Huston (Eds.), *Social exchanges in developing relationships* (pp. 135-168). New York: Academic Press.

Bratman, M. (1987). *Intentions, plans, and practical reasons*. Cambridge, MA: Harvard University Press.

Bryan, S. P., Berkos, K. M., Ross, S. H., & Croghan, J. M. (2000, August). *Banking on it: Imagined interactions in the workplace*. Paper presented at the annual Louisiana Communication Association Conference, Monroe, LA.

Buller, D. B., & Burgoon, J. K. (1993). Deception: Strategic and nonstrategic communication. In J. A. Daly & J. M. Wiemann (Eds.), *Strategic interpersonal communication* (pp. 191-223). Hillsdale, NJ: Erlbaum.

Buller, D. B., Strzyzewski, K., & Comstock, J. (1991). Interpersonal deception: I: Deceivers' reactions to receivers' suspicions and probing. *Communication Monographs, 58*, 1-24.

Burke, R. J. (1996). Performance evaluation and counseling in a professional firm. *Leadership & Organization Development Journal, 17*, 21-27.

Cane, D.B., & Gotlib, I.H. (1985). Implicit conceptualizations of depression: Implications for an interpersonal perspective. *Social Cognition, 3*, 341-368.

Cappella, J. N. (1985). The management of conversation. In M. L. Knapp & G. R. Miller (Eds.), *Handbook of interpersonal communication* (pp. 393-438). Thousand Oaks, CA: Sage.

Cappella, J. N. (1987). Interpersonal communication: Definitions and fundamental questions. In C. R. Berger & S. H. Chaffee (Eds.), *Handbook of communication science* (pp. 184-238). Thousand Oaks, CA: Sage.

Carnelley, K. B., & Janoff-Bulman, R (1992). Optimism about love relationships: General vs. specific lessons from one's personal experiences. *Journal of Social and Personal Relationships, 9*, 5-20.

Cartwright, R. D. (1984). Broken dreams: A study of the effects of divorce and depression on dream content. *Psychiatry, 47,* 251-259.

Caughey, J. L. (1984). *Imaginary social worlds.* Lincoln: University of Nebraska Press.

Cloven, D. H., & Roloff, M. E. (1991). Sense-making activities and interpersonal conflict: Communicative cues for the mulling blues. *Western Journal of Speech Communication, 55,* 134-158.

Cloven, D. H., & Roloff, M. E. (1993). The chilling effects of aggressive potential on the expression of complaints in intimate relationships. *Communication Monographs, 60,* 199-219.

Cohen, S., & Wills, T. A. (1985). Stress, social support, and the buffering hypothesis. *Psychological Bulletin, 98,* 310-357.

Collins, K., & Bell, R. (1997). Personality and aggression: The dissipation-rumination scale. *Personality and Individual Differences, 22,* 751-755.

Crawford, M. (1989). Humor in conversational context: Beyond biases in the study of gender and humor. In R. K. Unger (Ed.), *Representations: Social constructions of gender* (pp. 155-164). New York: Baywood.

Cronkhite, G. (1976). *Communication and awareness.* Menlo Park, CA: Cummings.

Crystal, S. (1984). Homeless men and homeless women: The gender gap. *Urban and Social Change Review, 17,* 2-6.

Daly, J. A., Vangelisti, A. L., & Daughton, S. M. (1987). The nature and correlates of conversational sensitivity. *Human Communication Research, 14,* 167-202.

Daun, A. (1991). Individualistic and collectivity among Swedes. *Ethos, 56,* 165-172.

Dewey, J. (1922) *Human nature and conduct: An introduction to social psychology.* New York: Henry Holt.

Doi, T. S. (1973). The Japanese patterns of communication and the concept of amae. *Quarterly Journal of Speech, 59,* 180-185.

Duck, S. (1980). Personal relationships in the 1980s: Towards an understanding of complex human sociality. *Western Journal of Speech Communication, 44,* 114-119.

Edwards, R., Honeycutt, J. M., & Zagacki, K. S. (1988). Imagined interaction as an element of social cognition. *Western Journal of Speech Communication, 52,* 23-45.

Edwards, R., Honeycutt, J. M., & Zagacki, K. S. (1989). Gender differences in imagined interactions. *Sex Roles, 21,* 259-268.

Farnsworth, J., Pett, M. A., & Lund, D. A. (1989). Predictors of loss management and well-being in later life widowhood and divorce. *Journal of Family Issues, 10,* 102-121.

Feeney, J. A., & Noller, P. (1991). Attachment style and verbal descriptions of romantic partners, *Journal of Social and Personal Relationships, 8,* 187-215.

Fincham, F. D., & Bradbury, T. N. (1989). The impact of attributions in marriage: An individual difference analysis. *Journal of Social and Personal Relationships, 6,* 69-85.

Fisher, H. (1994). The natural history of monogamy, adultery and divorce. New York: Fawcett.

Fitzpatrick, M. A. (1988). *Between husbands and wives*. Newbury Park, CA: Sage.

Floyd, F. J. (1988). Couples' reactions to communication behaviors. *Journal of Marriage and The Family, 50*, 523-532.

Fontenot, K. (1997, April). *Catching the liar: The effects of imagined interaction and information processing on deception detection*. Paper presented at the annual Southern States Communication Association Convention, Savannah, GA.

Freud, S. (1958). *The dynamics of transference (Standard Edition), 12*, 99-108. London: Hogarth. (Original work published 1912)

Frith, K. T., & Wesson, D. (1991). A comparison of cultural values in British and American print advertising: A study of magazines. *Journalism Quarterly, 68*, 216-223.

Furnham, A. (1987). The adjustment of sojourners. In Y. Y. Kim & W. B. Gudykunst (Eds.), *Cross-cultural adaptation: Current approaches* (pp. 126-143). Beverly Hills, CA: Sage.

Furnham, A., & Alibhai, N. (1985). The friendship networks of foreign students: A replication and extension of the functional model. *International Journal of Psychology, 20,* 709-722.

Gallegher, D. E., Thompson, L. W., & Peterson, J. A. (1981-1982). Psychosocial factors affecting adaptation to bereavement in the elderly. *International Journal of Aging and Human Development, 14,* 79-95.

Gallup, G., & Lindsay, M. D. (1999). *Surveying the religious landscape: Trends in U.S. beliefs*. Harrisburg, PA: Morehouse.

Galvin, K. M., & Brommel, B. J. (1986). *Family communication*. Glenview, IL: Scott, Foresman.

Gelles, R. J., & Straus, M. A. (1988). *Intimate violence*. New York: Simon & Schuster.

Gendrin, D. M. (1991). An intrapersonal process in cross-cultural adaptation: Imagined interactions among temporary sojourners. In R. G. Kunzendorf (Ed.), *Mental imagery* (pp. 129-138). New York: Plenum.

Gendrin, D. M. (1992, April). *The language function of imagined interactions in the process of cross-cultural adaptation*. Paper presented at the Southern Speech Communication Association Convention, San Antonio, TX.

Gendrin, D. M. (2000a, November). *Imagined interactions as a cognitive strategy in second language acquisition: A theoretical perspective*. Paper presented at the annual National Communication Association Convention, Seattle.

Gendrin, D. M. (2000b). Homeless' women's inner voices: Friends or foes? In M. Hardman & A. Taylor (Eds.), *Hearing many voices* (pp. 203-220). Cresskill, NJ: Hampton Press.

Gendrin, D. M., & Werner, B. L. (1996-1997). Internal dialogues about marital conflict: Implications for managing marital discord. *Imagination, Cognition, and Personality, 16*, 125-138.

Giambra, L. M. (1980). A factor analysis of the items of the Imaginal Processes Inventory. *Journal of Clinical Psychology, 36*, 383-409.

Gilligan, S. G., & Bower, G. H. (1984). Cognitive consequences of emotional arousal. In C. E. Izard, J. Kagan, & R. B. Zajonc (Eds.), *Emotions, cognition, and behavior* (pp. 547-588). Cambridge: Cambridge University Press.

Girard, M., & Mullet, E. (1997). Propensity to forgive in adolescents, young adults, older adults, and elderly people. *Journal of Adult Development, 4*, 209-220.

Gold, S. R., Gold, R., Milner, J. S., & Robertson, K. R. (1986-1987). Daydreaming and mental health. *Imagination, Cognition, and Personality, 6*, 67-74.

Goldstein, A.J., & Chambless, D.L. (1978). A re-analysis of agoraphobia. *Behavior Therapy, 9*, 47-59.

Gordon, W. J. (1961). *Syntectics: The development of creative capacity.* New York: Harper & Row.

Gorsuch, R. L., & Hao, J. Y. (1993). Forgiveness: An exploratory factor analysis and its relationship to religious variables. *Review of Religious Research, 34*, 333-347.

Gotcher, J. M., & Edwards, R. (1990). Coping strategies of cancer patients: Actual communication and imagined interactions. *Health Communication, 2*, 255-266.

Gotcher, J. M., & Honeycutt, J. M. (1989). An analysis of imagined interactions of forensic participants. *National Forensic Journal, 7*, 1-20.

Gottman, J. M. (1994). *What predicts divorce?* Hillsdale, NJ: Erlbaum.

Greene, J. O. (1984). A cognitive approach to human communication: An action-assembly theory. *Communication Monographs, 51*, 289-306.

Greer, S., Moorey, S., & Watson, M. (1989). Patients' adjustment to cancer: The mental adjustment to cancer (MAC) scale vs. clinical rating. *Journal of Psychometric Research, 33*, 373-377.

Gudykunst, W. B. (1988). Uncertainty and anxiety. In Y. Y. Kim & W. B. Gudykunst (Eds.), *Theories in intercultural communication.* Newbury Park, CA: Sage.

Harvey, J. H., Flannery, R., & Morgan, M. (1986). Vivid memories of vivid loves gone by. *Journal of Social and Personal Relationships, 3*, 359-373.

Hatfield, E. (1982). Passionate love, companionate love, and intimacy. In M. Fisher & G. Strickler (Eds.), *Intimacy* (pp. 267-292). New York: Plenum.

Hazan, C., & Shaver, P. (1987). Romantic love conceptualized as an attachment process. *Journal of Personality and Social Psychology, 52*, 511-524.

Hecht, M. (1978). The conceptualization and measurement of interpersonal communication satisfaction. *Human Communication Research, 4*, 253-264.

Hoffman, L. (1988). The family life cycle and discontinuous change. In B. Carter & M. MeGoldrick (Eds.), *The changing family life cycle* (pp. 91-105). New York: Gardner.

Honeycutt, J. M. (1989a). A functional analysis of imagined interaction activity in everyday life. In J. E. Shorr, P. Robin, J. A. Connelia, & M. Wolpin (Eds.), *Imagery: Current perspectives* (pp. 13-25). New York: Plenum.

Honeycutt, J. M. (1989b). A pilot analysis of imagined interaction accounts in the elderly. In R. Marks & J. Padgett (Eds.), *Louisiana: Health and the elderly* (pp. 183-201). New Orleans, LA: Pan American Life Center.

Honeycutt, J. M. (1991). Imagined interactions, imagery and mindfulness/mindlessness. In R. Kunzendorf (Ed.), *Mental imagery* (pp. 121-128). New York: Plenum.

Honeycutt, J. M. (1992). Components and functions of communication during initial interaction with extrapolations to beyond. In S. Deetz (Ed.), *Communication Yearbook 16* (pp. 461-514). Newbury Park, CA: Sage.

Honeycutt, J. M. (1995a). Imagined interactions, recurrent conflict and thought about personal relationships: A memory structure approach. In J. E. Aitken & L. J. Shedletsky (Eds.), *Intrapersonal communication processes* (pp. 138-150). Plymouth, MI: Speech Communication Association and Midnight Oil Multimedia.

Honeycutt, J. M. (1995b). The oral history interview and reports of imagined interactions. *Journal of Family Psychotherapy, 6,* 63-69.

Honeycutt, J. M. (1999a). Differences in imagined interactions as a consequence of marital ideology and attachment. *Imagination, Cognition, and Personality, 18,* 269-283.

Honeycutt, J. M. (1999b). Typological differences in predicting marital happiness from oral history behaviors and imagined interactions. *Communication Monographs, 66,* 276-291.

Honeycutt, J. M., & Brown, R. (1998). Did you hear the one about? Typological and spousal differences in the planning of jokes and sense of humor in marriage. *Communication Quarterly, 46,* 1-11.

Honeycutt, J. M., & Cantrill, J. C. (2001). *Cognition, communication, and romantic relationships.* Mahwah, NJ: Erlbaum.

Honeycutt, J. M., & Eidenmuller, M. E. (2001). An exploration of the effects of music and mood on intimate couples' verbal and nonverbal conflict-resolution behaviors. In V. Manusov & J. H. Harvey (Eds.), *Attribution, communication behavior, and close relationships* (pp. 37-60). London: Cambridge University Press.

Honeycutt, J. M., Edwards, R., & Zagacki, K. S. (1989-1990). Using imagined interaction features to predict measures of self-awareness: Loneliness, locus of control, self-dominance, and emotional intensity. *Imagination, Cognition, and Personality, 9,* 17-31.

Honeycutt, J. M., & Ford, S. G. (2001). Mental imagery and intrapersonal communication: A review of research on imagined interactions (IIs) and current developments. In W. B. Gudykunst (Ed.), *Communication yearbook 25* (pp. 315-345). Mahwah, NJ: Erlbaum.

Honeycutt, J. M., & Gotcher, J. M. (1991). Influence of imagined interactions on communicative outcomes: The case of forensic competition. In R. Kunzendorf (Ed.), *Mental imagery* (pp. 139-143). New York: Plenum Press.

Honeycutt, J. M., & McCann, R. (2001, November). *Predicting horizontal and vertical dimensions of individualism and collectivism in the Pacific Rim on the basis of imagined interactions.* Paper presented at the annual National Communication Association Convention, Atlanta, GA.

Honeycutt, J. M., & Patterson, J. (1997). Affinity strategies in relationships: The role of gender and imagined interactions in maintaining liking among college roommates. *Personal Relationships, 4,* 35-46.

Honeycutt, J. M., & Wiemann, J. M. (1999). Analysis of functions of talk and reports of imagined interactions (IIs) during engagement and marriage. *Human Communication Research, 25,* 399-419.

Honeycutt, J. M., Zagacki, K. S., & Edwards, R. (1989). Intrapersonal communication and imagined interactions. In C. Roberts & K. Watson (Eds.), *Readings in intrapersonal communication processes: Original essays* (pp. 167-184). Scottsdale, AZ: Gorsuch Scarisbrick.

Honeycutt, J. M., Zagacki, K. S., & Edwards, R. (1992-1993). Imagined interaction, conversational sensitivity and communication competence. *Imagination, Cognition, and Personality, 12,* 139-157.

Ifert, D. E., & Roloff, M. E. (1994). Anticipated obstacles to compliance: Predictors of their presence and expression. *Communication Studies, 45,* 120-130.

Infante, D. A. (1995). Teaching students to understand and control verbal aggression. *Communication Education, 44,* 51-63.

Infante, D. A., Chandler, T. A., & Rudd, J. E. (1989). Test of an argumentative skill deficiency model of interpersonal violence. *Communication Monographs, 56,* 163-177.

Infante, D. A., & Rancer, A. S. (1982). A conceptualization and measure of argumentativeness. *Journal of Personality Assessment, 46,* 72-80.

Infante, D. A., & Rancer, A. S. (1996). Argumentativeness and verbal aggressiveness: A review of recent theory and research. In B. Burleson (Ed.), *Communication Yearbook 19* (pp. 319-351). Thousand Oaks, CA: Sage.

Infante, D. A., Rancer, A. S., & Womack, D. F. (1997). *Building communication theory* (3rd ed.). Prospect Heights, IL: Waveland.

Infante, D. A., & Wigley, C. J. (1986). Verbal aggressiveness: An interpersonal model and measure. *Communication Monographs, 53,* 61-69.

Infoseek. (1998). [On line] Available at www.infoseek.com.

Johnson, D. M., Parrott, G. L., & Stratton, R. P. (1968). Production and judgment of solutions to five problems. *Journal of Educational Psychology, 59,* Monograph Supplement No. 6.

Johnson, K. L., & Roloff, M. E. (1998). Serial arguing and relational quality: Determinants and consequences of perceived resolvability. *Communication Research, 25,* 327-343.

Jones, E. E., & Gerard, H. B. (1967). *Foundations of social psychology.* New York: Wiley.

Kearney, P., Plax, T. G., Hays, E. R., & Ivey, M. J. (1991). College teacher misbehaviors: What students don't like about what teachers say and do. *Communication Quarterly, 39,* 309-324.

Kim, M. S. (1993). Culture-based interactive constraints in explaining cross-cultural strategic competence. In R. L. Wiseman & J. Koestler (Eds.), *International and intercultural communication annual 17* (pp. 132-150). Newbury Park: Sage.

Kim, M. S., Triandis, H. C., Kagitcibasi, C., & Yoon, G. (Eds.), (1994). *Individualism and collectivism: Theoretical and methodological issues.* Newbury Park, CA: Sage.

Kim, Y. Y. (1988). *Communication and cross-cultural adaptation: An integrative theory.* Clevedon, England: Multilingual Matters.

Klineberg, O., & Hull, W. (1979). *At a foreign university: An international study of adaptation and coping.* New York: Praeger.

Klinger, E. (1977). Consequences of commitment to and disengagement from incentives. *Psychological Review, 82,* 1-25.

Klinger, E. (1978). Modes of normal consciousness. In K. S. Pope & J. L. Singer (Eds.), *The stream of consciousness: Scientific investigations into the flow of human experience* (pp. 225-258). New York: Plenum.

Klinger, E. (1981). The central place of imagery in human functioning. In E. Klinger (Ed.), *Imagery: Concepts, results, and applications* (Vol. 2, pp. 3-16). New York: Plenum.

Klinger, E. (1987). Current concerns and disengagement from incentives. In F. Halisch & J. Kuhl (Eds.), *Motivation, intention and volition* (pp. 337-347). Berlin: Springer-Verlag.

Klinger, E. (1990). *Daydreaming.* Los Angeles, CA: Jeremy P. Tarcher.

Klos, D. S., & Singer, J. L. (1981). Determinants of the adolescent's ongoing thought following simulated parental confrontations. *Journal of Personality and Social Psychology, 41,* 975-987.

Knapp, M. L., & Comadena, M. (1979). Telling it like it isn't: A review of theory and research on deceptive communication. *Human Communication Research, 5,* 270-285.

Konrad, W. (1985). How to criticize an employee. *Working Woman, 10,* 22-23.

Krashen, S., & Scarcena, R. (1978). On routines and patterns in language acquisition and performance. *Language Learning, 28,* 283-300.

Kroeber, A. L., & Kluckhohn, C. (1952). *Culture: A critical review of concepts and definitions* (Papers of the Peabody Museum of Archaeology and Ethnology, Vol. 47, No. 1). Cambridge, MA: Peabody Museum.

Kroll-Mensing, D. (1992). *Differentiating anxiety and depression: An experience sampling analysis.* Unpublished doctoral dissertation, University of Minnesota, Minneapolis.

Langer, E. (1989). *Mindfulness.* Reading, MA: Addison Wesley.

Langer, E. J., Blank, A., & Chanowitz, B. (1978). The mindlessness of ostensibly thoughtful action: The role of placebic information in interpersonal interaction. *Journal of Personality and Social Psychology, 36,* 635-642.

Langer, E. J., Chanowitz, B., & Blank, A. (1985). Mindlessness-mindfulness in perspective: A reply to Valerie Folkes. *Journal of Personality and Social Psychology, 48,* 605-607.

Latty-Mann, H., & Davis, K. E. (1996). Attachment theory and partner choice: Preference and actuality. *Journal of Social and Personal Relationships, 13,* 5-24.

Levy, S. M., Herberman, R. B., Maluish, A. M., Schilen, B., & Lippman, M. (1985). Prognostic risk assessment in primary breast cancer by behavioral and immunological parameters. *Health Psychology, 4,* 99-113.

Lipset, S. M. (1963). *The first new nation: The United States in historical and comparative perspective.* New York: Basic Books.

Lopata, H. Z. (1973). Self-identity in marriage and widowhood. *Sociological Quarterly, 14,* 407-418.

Lopata, H. Z. (1975). On widowhood: Grief work and identity reconstruction. *Journal of Geriatric Psychiatry, 8,* 41-55.

Lord, C. (1979). Schemas and images as memory aids: Two models of processing social information. *Journal of Personality and Social Psychology, 38,* 674-687.

Lowenstein, A., Landau, R., & Rosen, A. (1993-94). Adjustment to loss of spouse as a multivariate construct. *Omega, 28,* 229-245.

Lyubomirsky, S., Tucker, K. L., Caldwell, N. D., & Berg, K. (1999). Why ruminators are poor problem solvers: Clues from the phenomology of dysphoric rumination. *Journal of Personality and Social Psychology, 77,* 1041-1060.

Makela, S. (1992, April). *The production, planning, and rehearsal of verbally aggressive messages in proactive imagined interactions.* Paper presented at the annual conference of the Central States Communication Association, Cleveland, OH.

Manis, J.G., & Meltzer, B.N. (1978). *Symbolic interaction: A reader in social psychology.* Boston: Allyn & Bacon.

Markus, H., & Kitayamma, S. (1991). Culture and self: Implications for cognition, emotion, and motivation. *Psychological Review, 98,* 228-253.

Markus, H., & Kitayamma, S. (1994). A collective fear of the collective: Implications for selves and theories of selves. *Personality and Social Psychology Bulletin, 20,* 568-579.

Marston, W. M. (1920). Reaction-time symptoms of deceptions. *Journal of Experimental Psychology, 3,* 72-87.

McCall, G. H., & Simmons, T. (1978). *Identities and interaction* (rev. ed.). New York: The Free Press.

McCornack, S. A., & Parks, M. R. (1986). Deception detection and relationship development: The other side of trust. In M. L. McLaughlin (Ed.), *Communication yearbook 9* (pp. 357-389). Beverly Hills, CA: Sage.

McCrosky, J. C. (1997, November). *Why we communicate the ways we do: A communibiological perspective.* Speech delivered for The Carroll C. Arnold Distinguished Lecture of the annual convention of the National Communication Association, Chicago, IL.

McCullough, M. E., Rachal, K. C., Sandage, S. J., Worthington, E. L., Jr., Brown, S. W., & Hight, T. L. (1998). Interpersonal forgiving in close relationships: II. Theoretical elaboration and measurement. *Journal of Personality and Social Psychology, 75,* 1586-1603.

McCune, J. (1997). Employee appraisals the electronic way. *Management Review, 26,* 44-48.

Mead, G. H. (1934). *Mind, self and society.* Chicago: University of Chicago Press.

Meyer, J. R. (1997). Cognitive influences on the ability to address interaction goals. In J. O. Greene (Ed.), *Message production: Advances in communication theory* (pp. 71-90). Mahwah, NJ: Erlbaum.

Murphy, C. M., & O'Farrell, S. (1994). Factors associated with marital aggression in male alcoholics. *Journal of Family Psychology, 8,* 321-335.

Myers, D. G., & Diener, E. (1995). Who is happy? *Psychological Science, 6,* 10-19.

Nolen-Hoeksema, S. (1991). Responses to depression and their effects on the duration of depressive episodes. *Journal of Abnormal Psychology, 100,* 569-582.

Nunnally, J. C. (1978). *Psychometric theory* (2nd ed.). New York: McGraw-Hill.

O'Malley, J. M., & Chamot, A. U. (1999). *Learning strategies in second-language acquisition.* Cambridge, MA: Cambridge University Press.

Osborn, A. F. (1953). Applied imagination. New York: Scribners.

Patterson, M. L. (1983). *Nonverbal behavior: A functional perspective.* New York: Springer-Verlag.

Patterson, M. L. (1987). Presentational and affect-management functions of nonverbal involvement. *Journal of Nonverbal Behavior, 11,* 110-122.

Pearce, W. B., & Cronen, V. E. (1980). *Communication, action, and meaning: The creation of social realities.* New York: Praeger.

Petress, K. C. (1990, June). *The role imagined interactions played in the Tian-an-men Square student demonstrations: An analysis of participants' self-reporting.* Paper presented at American Association for the Study of Mental Imagery, University of Massachusetts-Lowell, MA.

Petress, K. C. (1995). Coping with a new educational environment: Chinese students' imagined interactions before commencing studies in the U.S. *Journal of Instructional Psychology, 22,* 50-63.

Pfefferbaum, B., & Wood, P. B. (1994). Self-report study of impulsive and delinquent behavior in college students. *Journal of Adolescent Health, 15,* 295-302.

Phillips, N., & Brown, J. L. (1993). Analyzing communication in and around organizations: A critical hermeneutic approach. *Academy of Management Journal, 36,* 1547-1576.

Poole, M. S., & Folger, J. P. (1981). A method for establishing the representational validity of interaction coding systems: Do we see what they see? *Human Communication Research, 8,* 26-42.

Radley, A., & Green, R. (1987). Illness as adjustment: A methodology and conceptual framework. *Sociology of Health and Illness, 9,* 179-207.

Richmond, V. P., McCroskey, J. C., & Davis, L. M. (1986). The relationship of supervisor use of power and affinity-seeking strategies with subordinate satisfaction. *Communication Quarterly, 34*, 179-193.

Roloff, M. E., & Berger, C. R. (1982). Social cognition and communication: An introduction. In M. E. Roloff & C. R. Berger (Eds.), *Social cognition and communication* (pp. 9-32). Beverly Hills, CA: Sage.

Roloff, M. E., & Ifert, D. E. (1998). Exploring the role of private speech, imagined interaction, and serial interaction in mutual influence. In M. T. Palmer & G. A. Barnett (Eds.), *Progress in communication sciences* (Vol. 14, pp. 113-133). Stanford, CT: Ablex.

Romberger, B. V. (1986). Aunt Sophie always said . . . Oral histories of the commonplaces women learned about relating to men. *American Behavioral Scientist, 29*, 342-367.

Rook, K. S. (1988). Toward a more differentiated view of loneliness. In S. W. Duck (Ed.), *Handbook of personal relationships* (pp. 571-589). London: Wiley.

Rosenblatt, P. C., & Meyer, C. J. (1986). Imagined interactions and the family. *Family Relations, 35*, 319-324.

Rosenblatt, P. C., Meyer, C. J., & Karis, T. A. (1991-1992). Internal interactions with God. *Imagination, Cognition, and Personality, 11*, 85-97.

Rotter, J. B. (1975). Some problems and misconceptions related to the construct of internal versus external control of reinforcement. *Journal of Consulting and Clinical Psychology, 43*, 56-67.

Salters, L. (1997). Coaching and counseling for peak performance. *Business & Economic Review, 14*, 26-28.

Sanford, K. (1997). Two dimensions of adult attachment: Further validation. *Journal of Social and Personal Relationships, 14*, 133-143.

Schank, R. C. (1982). *Dynamic memory.* New York: Cambridge University Press.

Schultz, K. D. (1978). Imagery and the control of depression. In J. L. Singer & K. S. Pope (Eds.), *The power of human imagination.* New York: Plenum.

Schutz, A. (1962). Choosing among projects of action. In M. Natanson (Ed.), *Collected Papers, Vol. I: The problem of social reality* (pp. 67-96). The Hague, Netherlands: Martinus Nijhoff.

Schutz, W. C. (1958). *FIRO: A three-dimension theory of interpersonal behavior.* New York: Holt, Rinehart & Winston.

Schwartz, S. H. (1990). Individualism-collectivism: Critique and proposed refinements. *Journal of Cross-Cultural Psychology, 21*, 139-157.

Sherman, S. J., & Corty, E. (1984). Cognitive heuristics. In R. S. Wyer, Jr. & T. K. Srull (Eds.), *Handbook of social cognition* (Vol. 1). Hillsdale, NJ: Erlbaum.

Shweder, R. A. (1979). Beyond self-constructed knowledge: The study of culture and morality. *Merrill Palmer Quarterly, 28*, 41-69.

Singelis, T. M. (1994). Bridging the gap between culture and communication. In A-M. Bouvy, F. J. R. van de Vijver, P. Boski, & P. Schmitz (Eds.), *Journeys into cross-cultural psychology* (pp. 278-293). Lisse: Swets & Zeitlinger.

Singelis, T. M., & Brown, W. J. (1995). Culture, self, and collectivist communication: Linking culture to individual behavior. *Human Communication Research, 21,* 354-389.

Singelis, T. M., Triandis, H. C., Bhawuk, D. P. S., & Gelfand, M. J. (1995). Horizontal and vertical dimensions of individualism and collectivism: A theoretical and measurement refinement. *Cross-Cultural Research, 29,* 240-275.

Singer, J. L. (1985). *Private experience and public action: The study of ongoing thought.* Henry A. Murray Lecture, Symposium on Personality, Symposium conducted at Michigan State University, East Lansing.

Singer, J. L. (1987). Reinterpreting the transference. In D. C. Turk & P. Salovey (Eds.), *Reasoning, inference and judgment in clinical psychology* (pp. 182-205). New York: The Free Press.

Smeijsters, H. (1995). The functions of music in music therapy. In T. Wigram, B. Saperston, & R. West (Eds.), *The art and science of music therapy: A handbook* (pp. 385-394). Chur, Switzerland: Harwood Academic .

Spierer, H. (1981). Life cycle. In A. C. Eurich (Ed.), *Major transitions in the human life cycle* (pp. 7-59). Lexington, MA: D.C. Heath.

Stainton, M. C. (1985). The fetus: A growing member of the family. *Family Relations, 34,* 319-326.

Steiner, J. (1976). Some aspects of interviewing technique and their relationship with the transference. *British Journal of Medical Psychology, 49,* 65-72.

Stephen, T. (1984). A symbolic exchange framework for the development of intimate relationships. *Human Relations, 37,* 393-408.

Straus, M. A. (1990). Measuring intrafamily conflict: The conflict tactics (CTS) scales. In M. A. Straus & R. J. Gelles (Eds.), *Physical violence in American families: Risk factors and adaptations to violence in 8,145 families* (pp. 29-45). New Brunswick, NJ: Transaction Books.

Stroul, N. A. (1992). A manager for all seasons. *Training, 29,* 53-57.

Stuckless, N., & Goranson, R. (1992). The vengeance scale: Development of a measure of attitudes toward revenge. *Journal of Social Behavior and Personality, 7,* 25-42.

Swann, W. B., Griffin, J. J., Predmore, S. C., & Gaines, B. (1987). The cognitive affective crossfire: When self-consistency confronts self-enhancement. *Journal of Personality and Social Psychology, 52,* 881-889.

Teasdale, J. D. (1983). Negative thinking in depression: Cause, effect, or reciprocal relationship? *Behavior Research and Therapy, 5,* 3-26.

Tesser, A., & Leone, C. (1977). Cognitive schemas and thought as determinants of attitude change. *Journal of Experimental Social Psychology, 13,* 340-356.

Thomas, D. A. (1981). *Advanced debate: Readings in theory, practice, and teaching.* Skokie, IL: National Textbook.

Tobin, J., Wu, D., & Davidson, D. (1989). *Preschool in three cultures.* New Haven, CT: Yale University Press.

Triandis, H. C. (1995). *Individualism and collectivism.* Boulder, CO: Westview.

Triandis, H. C., Chen, X. P., & Chan, D. K. S. (1998). Scenarios for the measurement of collectivism and individualism. *Journal of Cross-Cultural Psychology, 29,* 275-289.

Ueda, K. (1974). Sixteen ways to avoid saying "no" in Japan: A survey of the function and frequency of Japanese patterns of declining requests. In J. Condon & M. Saito (Eds.), *Intercultural encounters with Japan* (pp. 185-192). Tokyo: Simul.

Ventrigha, L. (1982). *Conversations with Miquel and Maria: How children learn a second language.* Reading, MA: Addison-Wesley.

Vygotsky, L. S. (1986). *Thought and language* (A. Kozulin, Trans.). Cambridge, MA: MIT Press.

Wanzer, M. B., Booth-Butterfield, M., & Booth-Butterfield, S. (1994, November). *Confirmation of behavioral differences in the production of humor.* Paper presented at the annual Speech Communication Association Conference, New Orleans.

Watzlawick, P., Beavin, J. H., & Jackson, D. D. (1967). *Pragmatics of human communication.* New York: Norton.

Weldon, E. (1984). Deindividuation, interpersonal affect, and productivity in laboratory task groups. *Journal of Applied Social Psychology, 14,* 469-485.

Wenburg, J., & Wilmot, W. (1973). *The personal communication process.* New York: Wiley.

Whorf, B. (1956). *Language, thought, and reality.* New York: Wiley.

Wilensky, R. (1983). *Planning and understanding.* Reading, MA: Addison-Wesley.

Williamson, L. K. (1980). Prayer as a special case of intrapersonal communication. *Religious Communication Today, 3,* 12.

Woods, B. L., & Edwards, R. (1990, April). *Intrapersonal communication and the family life cycle: Imagined interactions of parents and college-bound students.* Paper presented at the annual meeting of the Southern States Communication Association, Birmingham, AL.

Zagacki, K. S., Edwards, R., & Honeycutt, J. M. (1992). The role of mental imagery and emotion in imagined interaction. *Communication Quarterly, 40,* 56-68.

Zillmann, D. (1983). Transfer of excitation in emotional behavior. In J. T. Cacioppo & R. E. Petty (Eds.), *Social psychology: A sourcebook* (pp. 215-240). New York: Guilford Press.

Ziv, A., & Gadish, O. (1989). Humor and marital satisfaction. *Journal of Social Psychology, 129,* 759-768.

Zuckerman, M., Koestner, R., & Colella, M. (1985). Learning to detect deception from three communication channels. *Journal of Nonverbal Behavior, 9,* 188-194. 218

Author Index

SUBJECT INDEX